Willkommen beim letzten Band der *Wordmaster*-Reihe!

Wie in den bisherigen *Wordmaster*-Bänden gibt es wieder zwei Hauptbestandteile:

1. Die New Words

Für fast alle neuen Vokabeln der Schülerbände D5 und D6 (Erweiterte Ausgabe) gibt es einen Beispielsatz. Die neue Vokabel kannst du (in der richtigen Form) in die Lücke des Beispielsatzes eintragen. Beim Lesen des Satzes lässt sich oft schon erahnen, welche Vokabel gefragt ist. Falls nicht, lies einfach den entsprechenden deutschen Satz auf der rechten Seite – dort steht die gesuchte Vokabel fett gedruckt.

Für die endgültige Lösung kannst du im „Vocabulary"-Teil des Schülerbuchs nachschauen. Da die Reihenfolge der Vokabeln im *Wordmaster* dieselbe wie im Schülerbuch ist, eignet sich der *Wordmaster* auch ideal als Vokabelheft.

2. Die Übungen

Die meisten neuen, aber auch viele „alte" Vokabeln kommen in den vielseitigen Übungen immer wieder zur Anwendung – und die Übungen sind dabei oft ein echter Rätselspaß! So kannst du dir die Vokabeln auch auf lange Sicht besser merken.

Und nun ... viel Spaß beim Üben!

D5 Unit 1

New words ▸ pp. 6–7

What _____ are you? – I'm British.   Welche **Nationalität** haben Sie? – Ich bin Brite.

The Australian _____ is hot and dry.   Das australische **Hinterland** ist heiß und trocken.

Many Australian animals live in _____.   Viele australische Tiere leben **im Busch**.

There are trees and _____ in our garden.   In unserem Garten gibt es Bäume und **Büsche**.

He slept in a _____ in a small tent.   Er schlief in einem **Schlafsack** in einem kleinen Zelt.

I'll buy steaks and sausages for our _____.   Ich kaufe Steaks und Würstchen für unser **Grillfest**.

You can all sleep _____ my _____.   Ihr könnt alle **bei** mir **zu Hause** übernachten.

I didn't see him, and he didn't see me _____.   Ich sah ihn nicht, und er sah mich **auch nicht**.

What's _____ the tree? – Its age.   Was ist **das Besondere** an dem Baum? – Sein Alter.

1 Scrambled words: Australia

Die Buchstaben auf der linken Seite der Anzeigetafel ergeben Wörter, die etwas mit Australien zu tun haben. Trage die gefundenen Wörter in die mittlere Spalte der Tafel ein. Die Tipps helfen dir.

	✈	✈	TIP
1	ORANGAKO		a typical Australian animal
2	HET HUSB		where these animals live
3	KENAS		a dangerous animal
4	ETH TOKUCAB		the middle of Australia
5	GUNFIRS		a typical Australian sport
6	BEERBAUC		party with meat and sausages
7	TICORIVA		a state in Australia
8	CARRYPESSK		a very tall building
9	LEBERNOMU		a city in Australia

1

New words ▶ p. 8

There are 50 stars on the US _____ .	Auf der amerikanischen **Flagge** sind 50 Sterne.
The total _____ of the US is 9,629,091 km².	Die Gesamt**fläche** der USA beträgt 9.629.091 km².
The Sahara is a huge _____ .	Die Sahara ist eine riesige **Wüste**.
How nice – a cake in the _____ of a heart!	Wie nett – ein Kuchen in der **Form** eines Herzens!
The Swiss flag is red with a white _____ .	Die Schweizer Fahne ist rot mit weißem **Kreuz**.
Landing on the moon was a _____ event.	Die Mondlandung war ein **historisches** Ereignis.
Native Australians were called _____ .	Ureinwohner Australiens nannte man **Aborigines**.
Some _____ people still hunt in the bush.	Manche **Aborigines** jagen immer noch im Busch.
AIDS is a terrible _____ .	AIDS ist eine schlimme **Krankheit**.
Canada was once a British _____ .	Kanada war einmal eine britische **Kolonie**.
Two _____ have escaped from jail.	Zwei **Gefangene** sind aus dem Gefängnis geflohen.
He was sent to _____ for two years.	Er musste für zwei Jahre ins **Gefängnis** gehen.
Today India is _____ from Britain.	Indien ist heute **unabhängig** von Großbritannien.
Does the company _____ with China?	**Treibt** die Firma **Handel** mit China?

2 Definitions

Vervollständige die Definitionen mit Wörtern aus dem linken Display.
Trage die richtige Lösung aus dem anderen Display in die rechte Spalte ein.

area crime essay government jail land part place rain stamps

collection colony conclusion desert prisoner

1 a country or _area_ under the _____ of another country   _colony_

2 a person who is guilty of a _____ and is now in _____   _____

3 the final _____ of a speech or an _____   _____

4 a large area of _____ without much _____   _____

5 a group of pictures, _____ , etc. that someone has in one _____   _____

New words ▸ p. 9

Our cat always stays _____ at night.	Unsere Katze bleibt nachts immer **draußen**.
She stayed in _____ the bad weather.	Sie blieb zu Hause **wegen** des schlechten Wetters.
You can get _____ from smoking.	Vom Rauchen kann man **Krebs** bekommen.
She drove slowly to _____ an accident.	Sie fuhr langsam, um einen Unfall zu **vermeiden**.
Put on _____ when you lie in the sun!	Nimm **Sonnenschutzmittel** zum Sonnenbaden!
We saw lots of fish in the coral _____ .	Wir sahen viele Fische im Korallen**riff**.
A _____ is a very intelligent sea animal.	Ein **Delfin** ist ein sehr intelligentes Meerestier.
Moby Dick was a white _____ .	Moby Dick war ein weißer **Wal**.
The price of petrol went up _____ five cents.	Der Benzinpreis stieg **um** fünf Cent.
Her life has changed in _____ years.	Ihr Leben hat sich in **den letzten** Jahren verändert.
I saw Tim _____ – three days ago, I think.	**Neulich** sah ich Tim – vor drei Tagen, glaube ich.

3 More about ... Australia

Vervollständige den Text mit den passenden Wörtern aus der Box.

> Aboriginal – area – beaches – cancer – desert – independent –
> koala – population – snakes – sunscreen

Australia has an (1) _____ almost as large as Europe. But with 21.2 million people, Australia's (2) _____ is only about one quarter of Germany's! It was once a British colony, which became (3) _____ in 1901. Today, most people live in the big cities on the coast, while only a few Australians live in the bush or the (4) _____ .

A lot of people go to see Ayers Rock (or Uluru), which is a huge, red rock in the middle of Australia. The rock actually belongs to the (5) _____ people in that area. There is a path up the rock which tourists can climb.

Tourists love Australia because of the beautiful (6) _____ , fantastic countryside and interesting animals, like the kangaroo, the emu and the (7) _____ . But be careful: some animals are very dangerous, like (8) _____ or salt-water crocodiles. And you should avoid the sun. If you don't put on (9) _____ , you can easily get skin (10) _____ !

1

New words ▶ pp. 10–11

This _____ should be 7, not 10.5.	Diese **Zahl** sollte 7 und nicht 10,5 sein.
The _____ shows rising sales.	Das **Balkendiagramm** zeigt steigende Verkäufe.
This _____ compares four countries.	Dieses **Tortendiagramm** vergleicht vier Länder.
A high _____ of Germans have a car.	Ein hoher **Prozentsatz** der Deutschen hat ein Auto.
Let's _____ the cake into two halves.	Lass uns den Kuchen in zwei Hälften **aufteilen**.
Wait a minute! I've _____ finished.	Einen Moment! Ich bin **fast** fertig.
In autumn the _____ become yellow and red.	Im Herbst werden die **Blätter** gelb und rot.

4 Odd word out

*Ein Wort passt nicht.
Finde und unterstreiche es.*

1 tiger – dolphin – bear – lion

2 almost – about – nearly – recently

3 avoid – illness – disease – sick

4 reef – prison – fish – sea

5 Aborigine – the bush – outback – cross

6 figure – percentage – number – leaf

7 outback – outdoors – outside – open-air

8 nationality – shape – flag – country

5 Words with different meanings

*Finde auf der Liste (Seestern-Magnet) ein passendes Wort zu den beiden Sätzen/Satzteilen auf den Zetteln 1–6.
Trage es dort ein und unterstreiche die beiden deutschen Entsprechungen.*

1)
a) Im australischen Busch gibt es Schlangen.
b) Der Strauch hat gelbe Blätter.
bush

2)
a) die Fläche eines Landes
b) Sie wohnt in einer schönen Gegend.

3)
a) in der Gegenwart leben
b) Ich habe ein Geschenk für dich.

4)
a) Wir müssen den Fluss hier überqueren.
b) Auf der Kirche ist ein Kreuz.

5)
a) Der Baum hat keine Blätter.
b) Der Zug fährt um 10 Uhr ab.

area
bush
by
cross
leaves
present

6)
a) Die Preise stiegen um 5 Prozent.
b) Wir fahren mit dem Auto.

New words ▶ pp. 12–14

Turn around – this road goes _____.	Kehr um – diese Straße führt **nirgendwohin**.
Don't help me – I want to do it _____.	Hilf mir nicht – ich will das **allein** machen.
Never ride a _____ without a helmet.	Fahre nie **Motorrad** ohne Helm.
I'll _____ a photo to the e-mail.	Ich **hänge** ein Foto **an** die E-Mail.
Don't be a _____ – be more active!	Sei kein **Stubenhocker** – sei aktiver!
Things that you don't expect are _____.	Dinge, die man nicht erwartet, sind **überraschend**.
It's closed today. – Oh, _____. Thanks.	Es ist heute geschlossen. – **Ach so**. Danke.
This beach has a _____.	Dieser Strand hat eine **Rettungsschwimmerstation**.
The _____ told the police what he had seen.	Der **Zeuge** sagte der Polizei, was er gesehen hatte.
I need your _____: this shirt or that one?	Ich brauche deinen **Rat**: dieses Hemd oder das da?
I _____ you to change your job.	Ich **rate** dir, den Job zu wechseln.

6 Word pairs

Welche Wörter passen zusammen?

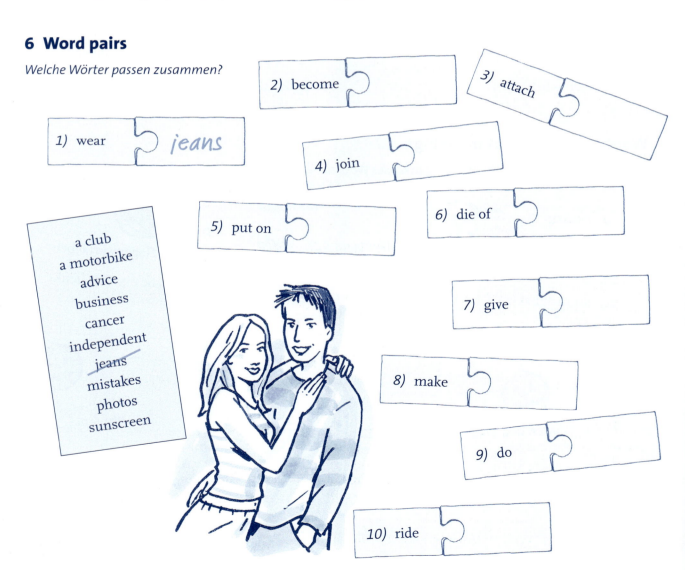

1) wear — jeans
2) become
3) attach
4) join
5) put on
6) die of
7) give
8) make
9) do
10) ride

a club
a motorbike
advice
business
cancer
independent
jeans
mistakes
photos
sunscreen

New words ▶ p. 15

Is this your own flat or do you _____ it?	Ist das deine Wohnung oder **mietest** du sie?
How much _____ do you pay for the flat?	Wie viel **Miete** zahlst du für die Wohnung?
Hi! _____? – Fine, thanks.	Hallo! **Wie geht's**? – Danke, gut.
Is this _____ free? – Yes, sit down, please.	Ist der **Platz** frei? – Ja, bitte setzt Dich.
May I _____ myself? My name's Sue.	Darf ich mich **vorstellen**? Ich heiße Sue.
Can I _____ your pen, please?	Kann ich deinen Stift **ausleihen**?
Don't worry! I can _____ you the money.	Keine Sorge! Ich kann dir das Geld **leihen**.

7 Word building

Verbinde die Wörter 1–10 mit jeweils einem passenden Wort aus der Mauer. Achte dabei auf die Schreibweise (getrennt oder zusammen), und trage die deutsche Übersetzung ein.

Wall words: ache, bag, bike, chart, guard, money, paper, potato, reef, table

1 coral **reef** — Korallenriff
2 life**guard** _____
3 pocket _____
4 pie _____
5 news _____
6 couch _____
7 stomach _____
8 motor _____
9 time _____
10 sleeping _____

8 Word friends

Auf jedem Plakat gibt es drei Wörter/Wortverbindungen, die direkt nach dem Verb auf dem kleinen Zettel folgen können. Unterstreiche sie.

do: the homework, a phone call, a good job, a mistake, business with sb.

wear: a bag, a cap, make-up, a camera, a ring

get: prison, advice, help, flag, cancer

have: a barbecue, percentage, witness, a disease, breakfast

8 | 1

New words ▶ p. 16

Holland is quite _____ – there are no hills.	Holland ist ziemlich **flach** – dort gibt es keine Hügel.
Uluru has _____ with Aboriginal paintings.	Uluru hat **Höhlen** mit Aborigine-Malereien.
Scotland is known for its beautiful _____.	Schottland ist bekannt für seine schöne **Landschaft**.
Do you know who's the _____ of this dog?	Weißt du, wer der **Besitzer** dieses Hundes ist?
Immigrants _____ in foreign countries.	Einwanderer **siedeln** in fremden Ländern.
The first _____ in America were Europeans.	Die ersten **Siedler** in Amerika waren Europäer.
We all share the _____ in human rights.	Wir alle teilen den **Glauben** an die Menschenrechte.
This family tree shows all my _____.	Dieser Stammbaum zeigt alle meine **Vorfahren**.
Biology is about _____ and animals.	In Biologie geht es um **Pflanzen** und Tiere.
After the fire we _____ lots of new trees.	Nach dem Feuer **pflanzten** wir viele neue Bäume.
I was ill. – Oh, _____ you didn't come.	Ich war krank. – Ah, **darum** bis du nicht gekommen.
You _____ drink lots of water when it's hot.	Du **musst** viel trinken, wenn es heiß ist.
I _____ your opinion, but I don't share it.	Ich **respektiere** deine Meinung, teile sie aber nicht.
He's strong, so they have _____ for him.	Er ist stark, daher haben sie **Respekt** vor ihm.

9 The best word

Finde das Wort A, B, C oder D, das am besten in die Lücke passt.

A	lend	B	rent
C	lie	D	borrow

1 Could I perhaps _____ some money from you?

A	amnesties	B	Aborigines
C	ancestors	D	actors

2 Some of the Queen's _____ are actually German.

A	settler	B	witness
C	owner	D	prisoner

3 My name's Fawlty – I'm the _____ of this hotel.

A	historical	B	untidy
C	unhappy	D	surprising

4 It's not _____ that the leaves are falling – it's autumn.

A	still	B	nearly
C	fast	D	recently

5 Look, it's _____ three o'clock! We're going to be late!

A	witness	B	prisoner
C	nationality	D	advice

6 There was no _____ to the crime.

A	advised	B	planted
C	segregated	D	settled

7 A lot of Europeans _____ in America.

A	chair	B	seat
C	place	D	space

8 There's only one empty _____ on the bus.

1

New words ▸ pp. 17–19

Does the older _____ use laptops?	Benutzt die ältere **Generation** Laptops?
He didn't like black people. He was a _____.	Er hatte etwas gegen Schwarze. Er war ein **Rassist**.
different _____ and ethnic groups	unterschiedliche **Rassen** und ethnische Gruppen
Her parents died young – she was an _____.	Ihre Eltern starben früh – sie war eine **Waise**.
Children should sit _____ of the car.	Kinder sollten **hinten** im Auto sitzen.
We can transport it by train or _____.	Wir können es per Bahn oder **LKW** transportieren.
It was so hot that I slept without a _____.	Es war so heiß, dass ich ohne **Decke** schlief.
I'd like to _____ for being late.	Ich möchte mich für die Verspätung **entschuldigen**.
'I'm sorry' is a short _____.	„Tut mir leid" ist eine kurze **Entschuldigung**.
He's healthy – he _____ his body.	Er ist gesund – er **nimmt** seinen Körper **wichtig**.
My garden has a rabbit-_____ fence.	Mein Garten hat einen kaninchen-**sicheren** Zaun.
I didn't get nervous – I stayed really _____.	Ich wurde nicht nervös – ich blieb ganz **ruhig**.
This _____ says that it's a great film.	In dieser **Filmkritik** steht, es sei ein toller Film.
Can you _____ a good restaurant?	Kannst du ein gutes Restaurant **empfehlen**?

10 Opposites

Trage das Gegenteil der fettgedruckten Wörter in die Lücken ein.

1 **borrow** / _____ some money
2 play **indoors** / _____
3 be **everywhere** / _____
4 a **nervous** / _____ student
5 a **hilly** / _____ landscape
6 have **old-fashioned** / _____ ideas
7 the **departure** / _____ of a train
8 a **slow** / _____ car
9 so **much** / _____ water
10 **falling** / _____ prices

11 open the **front** / _____ door
12 be **rich** / _____
13 drink **more** / _____ orange juice
14 **legal** / _____ immigrants
15 have an **advantage** / a _____
16 **push** / _____ a door
17 the answer is **right** / _____
18 a **clean** / _____ window
19 **forget** / _____ something
20 a **strong** / _____ man

New words ▸ pp. 20–21

It doesn't rain here often – just _____ . Es regnet hier nicht oft – nur **ab und zu.**

You can't _____ under water. Unter Wasser kann man nicht **atmen.**

After the 10 km run she was out of _____ . Nach dem 10-km-Lauf war sie außer **Atem.**

_____ your head if you want to say 'no'. **Schüttel** den Kopf, wenn du „nein" sagen willst.

She was wearing a medal around her _____ . Sie trug eine Medaille um den **Hals.**

My car won't go. Can you _____ it? Mein Auto fährt nicht. Kannst du es **reparieren?**

She was brave and showed no sign of _____ ! Sie war mutig und zeigte kein Anzeichen von **Angst!**

She put _____ in his food to kill him. Sie tat **Gift** in sein Essen, um ihn zu töten.

Don't eat that mushroom – it's _____ ! Iss diesen Pilz nicht – er ist **giftig!**

11 Spot the mistakes

In jedem Satz sind zwei Fehler. Unterstreiche und korrigiere sie.

1 It's terrible! <u>It gives</u> just too much cars in this city. *There are* _____

2 House prices fell at more than five percentage last year. _____ _____

3 I don't know how to introduce me. – I don't know, too. _____ _____

4 Can you borrow me an other pen? – Sure. You needn't ask. _____ _____

5 She had red hairs, like the leafs in autumn. _____ _____

6 Do the work on you own, but don't spent too much time on it. _____ _____

12 Making new words

Bilde aus den Buchstaben des Wortes so viele neue Wörter wie möglich. Mindestens 20 Wörter solltest du leicht finden. Wenn du über 50 findest, bist du ein „Buchstabenchampion".

anti, noise,

conversation

New words ▶ pp. 22–24

Sad stories _____ me cry.	Traurige Geschichten **bringen** mich **zum** Weinen.
There are lots of cows on the _____ farm.	Auf der **Rinder**farm gibt es viele Kühe.
She had a rucksack on her _____.	Sie trug einen Rucksack auf dem **Rücken**.
Careful! If you cut yourself, you'll _____.	Vorsicht! Wenn du dich schneidest, **blutest** du.
He was fully _____ during the operation!	Er war **bei** vollem **Bewusstsein** während der OP!
Now be _____ – did you take his money?	Sei mal **ehrlich** – hast du sein Geld genommen?
That's very _____ of you to help me.	Das ist sehr **nett**, dass du mir hilfst.

13 The fourth word

Welches Wort fehlt hier?

1 polite – rude   kind – _unkind_   6 danger – dangerous   poison – _____
2 feel – feeling   believe – _____   7 suitcase – hand   rucksack – _____
3 alive – dead   conscious – _____   8 land – elephant   sea – _____
4 pork – pigs   beef – _____   9 anything – nothing   anywhere – _____
5 life – live   breath – _____   10 breath – breathe   blood – _____

14 Pronunciation

Ordne die Wörter der beiden Rapper der richtigen Aussprachegruppe zu, je nachdem, wie der unterstrichene Vokal ausgesprochen wird.

ə   ɒ

colony (2)   _____

because of, b<u>o</u>rrow, <u>a</u>ncestor, h<u>o</u>nest, intr<u>o</u>duce, Ab<u>o</u>rigine, d<u>o</u>lphin, col<u>o</u>ny (2), pris<u>o</u>n, c<u>o</u>nscious, ap<u>o</u>logize (2), c<u>o</u>lony (1), hist<u>o</u>rical, cr<u>o</u>ss, pois<u>o</u>n, ap<u>o</u>logize (1)

D5 Unit 2

New words ▸ p. 32

Nobody knows what the _____ will bring.	Niemand weiß, was die **Zukunft** bringen wird.
_____ to become a teacher takes two years.	Die **Ausbildung** zum Lehrer dauert zwei Jahre.
At the age of 18 he _____ as an actor.	Mit 18 **machte** er eine Schauspiel**ausbildung**.
What kind of _____ is a GCSE?	Was für ein **Abschluss** ist ein GCSE?
She's doing an _____ as a hairdresser.	Sie macht eine **Lehre** als Frisörin.
As an _____, you learn at work.	Als **Lehrling** lernt man bei der Arbeit.
Choosing my job was a difficult _____.	Meine Berufswahl war eine schwere **Entscheidung**.
You need good language _____ for this job.	Du brauchst gute Sprach**fertigkeiten** für diesen Job.
A _____ stopped our car.	Ein **Polizist** hielt unser Auto an.
He's a fitness _____ in a sports centre.	Er ist Fitness**trainer** in einem Sportzentrum.
The _____ prepared her face.	Die **Maskenbildnerin** machte ihr Gesicht zurecht.
She's a _____ at our kindergarten.	Sie ist **Erzieherin** in unserem Kindergarten.
We want more _____ for small children.	Wir wollen mehr **Kinderbetreuung** für Kleinkinder.

1 The best word

Finde das Wort A, B, C oder D, das am besten in die Lücke passt.

A	instruction	B	apologies
C	apprentice	D	information

1 Go on the Internet to find more _____ about jobs.

A	get	B	do
C	make	D	catch

2 Let's stop the discussion – we have to _____ a decision now.

A	education	B	advice
C	training	D	way

3 You have to do special _____ to become a paramedic.

A	needn't	B	mustn't
C	haven't	D	don't need

4 You _____ have any special skills for this job.

A	earned	B	began
C	received	D	won

5 In 2010 he _____ an apprenticeship as a mechanic.

A	round	B	for
C	after	D	up

6 A childcare assistant looks _____ children.

A	skills	B	skirts
C	skins	D	sketches

7 What _____ do I need to do this job?

New words ▶ p. 33

The restaurant's _____ cooks excellently.	Der **Koch** des Restaurants macht tolles Essen.
The car _____ didn't find his tools.	Der Auto**mechaniker** fand sein Werkzeug nicht.
I need to take my car to the _____.	Ich muss mein Auto in die **Werkstatt** bringen.
A _____ knows all the products.	Ein **Kundenberater** kennt alle Produkte.
He's tired because he works _____.	Er ist müde, weil er **lange arbeitet**.
Please _____ this customer first.	Bitte **bediene** diesen Kunden zuerst.
This painter has lots of _____ talent.	Dieser Maler hat viel **künstlerisches** Talent.
The event was very well _____.	Die Veranstaltung war sehr gut **organisiert**.
The job is hard work, but the _____ is good.	Der Job ist schwer, aber die **Bezahlung** ist gut.

2 The fourth word

Welches Wort fehlt hier?

1 '3' – number   'B' – _____
2 reality – real   sport – _____
3 weak – strong   nervous – _____
4 relax – relaxed   organize – _____

5 cleverness – clever   art – _____
6 believe – belief   decide – _____
7 students – teach   customers – _____
8 music – musician   advice – _____

3 Lost words

Ergänze die Sätze mit der jeweils korrekten Präposition.
Bei zwei Sätzen bleibt die Lücke leer.

1 I've attached all the photos _____ my e-mail.
2 She failed the exam, but she was pretty relaxed _____ it.
3 Sorry, dear – I have to work _____ long hours again today.
4 Now let me give you an important piece _____ advice.
5 The teacher divided the class _____ four groups.
6 When he finally arrived, he apologized _____ being late.
7 What she said really made me _____ laugh.
8 The garage is closed _____ Monday.

2

New words ▶ p. 34

Please _____ the article on blue paper.	Bitte **drucke** den Artikel auf blauem Papier.
Can I _____ you _____ me a favour?	Kann ich dich **bitten**, mir einen Gefallen **zu tun**?
Take your time. I _____ waiting.	Lass dir Zeit. **Es macht mir nichts aus**, zu warten.
It's _____ to be tired after hard work.	Es ist **normal**, nach harter Arbeit müde zu sein.
Believe me – my source is very _____.	Glaub mir – meine Quelle ist sehr **zuverlässig**.
I have a problem which I can't _____.	Ich habe ein Problem, das ich nicht **lösen** kann.

4 Spot the mistakes

In jedem Satz sind zwei Fehler. Unterstreiche und korrigiere sie.

1 It's no problem – I don't mind to work long times in my job. _____ _____
2 He gave me some good advices on how to repare a car. _____ _____
3 As make-up artist you have to be calm and good organized. _____ _____
4 I've spended quite a lot of money for the new printer. _____ _____
5 What do you make in your job? – I'm serving people every day. _____ _____

5 Word pairs

Welche Wörter passen zusammen?

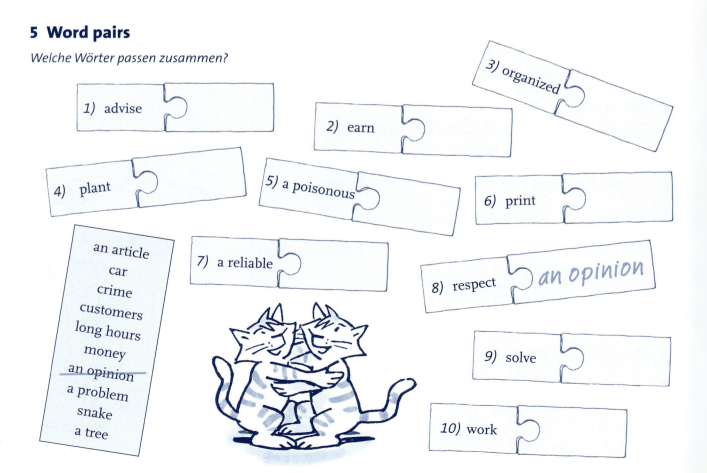

1) advise
2) earn
3) organized
4) plant
5) a poisonous
6) print
7) a reliable
8) respect — an opinion
9) solve
10) work

an article
car
crime
customers
long hours
money
~~an opinion~~
a problem
snake
a tree

New words ▸ p. 35

Our body is _____ made up of water.	Unser Körper besteht **hauptsächlich** aus Wasser.
She has all the _____ of a good teacher.	Sie hat alle **Eigenschaften** einer guten Lehrerin.
I don't feel _____ on a stage.	Ich fühle mich nicht **selbstsicher** auf einer Bühne.
The new boss is young and _____.	Die neue Chefin ist jung und **tatkräftig**.
Turn the light off – we need to save _____.	Mach das Licht aus – wir müssen **Energie** sparen.
My Porsche is as fast as a _____.	Mein Porsche ist so schnell wie ein **Rennwagen**.
She likes animals – she's a _____.	Sie mag Tiere – sie ist **Tierarzthelferin**.
Maths is easy. It's all very _____.	Mathe ist leicht. Alles ist sehr **logisch**.
Today, cars are full of modern _____.	Heute sind Autos voll mit moderner **Technologie**.
The computer _____ repaired my PC.	Der Computer**techniker** reparierte meinen PC.
The _____ finished the house in 1 year.	Die **Bauarbeiter** stellten das Haus in 1 Jahr fertig.
The bus was late, but the train was _____.	Der Bus kam zu spät, aber der Zug war **pünktlich**.
I never work outdoors – I'm an _____.	Ich arbeite nie draußen – ich bin **Büroangestellter**.
A _____ works in a hospital.	Eine **Krankenschwester** arbeitet im Krankenhaus.

6 Scrambled words: Describing people

Die Buchstaben auf der linken Seite der Anzeigetafel ergeben Wörter, mit denen man Menschen beschreiben kann. Trage die gefundenen Wörter in die mittlere Spalte der Tafel ein. Die Tipps helfen dir.

			TIP
1	CENTINDOF		believing in yourself
2	CENTIGERE		full of energy
3	LAMC		not nervous or excited
4	PYROTS		enjoying tennis, climbing, etc.
5	UPLUNACT		never late
6	CARSITTI		good at art
7	AREBELLI		always doing things correctly
8	COGALLI		combining facts when thinking

16 2

New words ▸ *pp. 36–37*

Yoga is boring – I have no _____ in it. Yoga ist langweilig – ich habe kein **Interesse** daran.

Write an _____ if you want the job. Schreib eine **Bewerbung**, wenn du den Job willst.

We had to _____ the whole worksheet! Wir mussten das ganze Arbeitsblatt **ausfüllen**!

You need to fill in an application _____. Du musst ein Bewerbungs**formular** ausfüllen.

You have to sign in _____, not in pencil. Du musst mit **Tinte** unterschreiben, nicht Bleistift.

We call each other by our _____ here. Wir nennen uns hier beim **Vornamen**.

Travis is both a first name and a _____. Travis ist sowohl Vorname als auch **Nachname**.

He did a week's _____ at a bank. Er machte ein einwöchiges **Praktikum** in der Bank.

It's the band's best song _____. Es ist das **bis heute** beste Lied der Band.

7 Word search: Jobs

Finde 21 Berufe und übersetze sie ins Deutsche. (↓ →)

S	X	A	F	A	R	M	E	R	H	J	D	E	N	T	I	S	T	Q	H
M	B	D	E	T	J	N	U	R	S	E	Z	P	P	A	I	N	T	E	R
E	B	O	B	U	I	L	D	E	R	Z	L	K	Z	L	P	D	C	E	T
C	J	C	A	P	H	K	L	N	C	H	E	F	M	N	C	N	L	L	E
H	M	T	C	A	J	F	Z	G	C	W	V	A	D	V	I	S	E	R	C
A	J	O	U	R	N	A	L	I	S	T	V	E	T	L	W	V	A	T	H
N	K	R	Z	A	G	L	B	N	X	I	Z	P	Y	M	B	B	N	E	N
I	Z	H	Q	M	L	U	B	E	D	I	T	O	R	K	P	I	E	A	I
C	Z	A	S	E	C	A	R	E	T	A	K	E	R	X	I	M	R	C	C
F	Z	C	Q	D	Y	F	I	R	E	M	A	N	R	H	L	B	W	H	I
T	F	K	L	I	C	L	G	Z	P	O	L	I	C	E	M	A	N	E	A
D	T	Q	A	C	T	O	R	Z	Z	K	G	D	X	T	Q	M	C	R	N

policeman – Polizist _____ _____

_____ _____ _____

_____ _____ _____

_____ _____ _____

_____ _____ _____

_____ _____ _____

New words ▸ p. 38 (part 1)

After school he _____ for a few jobs.	Nach der Schule **bewarb** er sich um einige Jobs.
Put these skills on your _____.	Schreib diese Fertigkeiten in deinen **Lebenslauf**.
How old is he? What's his date of _____?	Wie alt ist er? Was ist sein **Geburts**datum?
W5 2DU is the _____ of the London hotel.	W5 2DU ist die **Postleitzahl** des Londoner Hotels.
At the age of 11 you go to _____.	Mit 11 geht man auf die **weiterführende** Schule.
In _____ you learn to read and write.	In der **Grundschule** lernt man Lesen und Schreiben.
She gave _____ till an ambulance arrived.	Sie leistete **Erste Hilfe**, bis ein Krankenwagen kam.
After the course he got a _____.	Nach dem Kurs bekam er ein **Zertifikat**.
You can't drive a car with a _____.	Mit **Mopedführerschein** darf man nicht Auto fahren.
You mustn't drive without a _____.	Ohne **Führerschein** darf man nicht fahren.
She attached a _____ from her last job.	Sie hängte eine **Referenz** ihres letzten Jobs an.

8 Word families

a) Finde die passenden Verben zu den angegebenen Nomen.

1 breath – _____   *5* application – _____   *9* plant – _____

2 respect – _____   *6* training – _____   *10* blood – _____

3 belief – _____   *7* decision – _____   *11* rent – _____

4 advice – _____   *8* introduction – _____   *12* apology – _____

b) Vervollständige die Sätze mit der korrekten Form eines Verbs oder Nomens aus a).

1 You could at least _____ for being late!

2 Chris, can I _____ you to Sandra? She's an old friend.

3 I'm going to _____ more trees in the garden.

4 I decided to move – my _____ was too high.

5 The job sounded good, but I didn't _____ for it.

6 Just relax and _____ normally.

7 Their government doesn't _____ human rights.

8 After school I'd like to _____ as a paramedic.

18 **2**

New words ▸ pp. 38 (part 2)–39

I read your job _____ in *The Times*.	Ich habe Ihre Stellen**anzeige** in der *Times* gelesen.
Should beer be _____ on TV?	Sollte man im Fernsehen für Bier **werben**?
Don't forget to _____ your CV.	Vergiss nicht, deinen Lebenslauf **beizulegen**.
Leave the key at the hotel _____.	Lass den Schlüssel an der Hotel**rezeption**.
I'll be _____ to send you my references.	**Gerne** schicke ich Ihnen meine Referenzen.
Do you keep in _____ with old friends?	Bleibst du mit alten Freunden in **Kontakt**?
You can _____ her by phone or e-mail.	Man kann sie per Telefon oder Email **kontaktieren**.
Is this Harry Potter film _____ to the book?	Ist dieser Harry Potter Film **ähnlich** wie das Buch?
A _____ film is about plants and animals.	Ein **Natur**film handelt von Pflanzen und Tieren.
In _____ jobs you need to think logically.	In **technischen** Berufen muss man logisch denken.
He studied Maths at a technical _____.	Er studierte Mathe an einer beruflichen **Fachschule**.
My _____ of English? I'm a beginner.	Mein Englisch**niveau**? Ich bin Anfänger.

9 Odd word out

Ein Wort passt nicht. Finde und unterstreiche es.

1 school – nature – college – university

2 cattle – vet – nurse – builder

3 CV – postcode – reference – certificate

4 manager – leader – chef – boss

5 level – ambulance – paramedic – first aid

6 training – apprenticeship – ink – work experience

7 motorbike – racing car – garage – truck

8 reliable – punctual – organized – similar

10 Word stress

Unterstreiche bei allen Wörtern die Silbe, die betont werden muss.

address	advertise	advertisement	application
certificate	confident	decision	enclose
garage	indoors	nationality	nature
normal	organized	qualification	reference
reliable	similar	technical	technology

New words ▶ p. 40

The _____ went well – he got the job!	Das **Vorstellungsgespräch** lief gut – er hat den Job!
They gave the job to the other _____.	Sie gaben dem anderen **Bewerber** den Job.
His sports car didn't _____ her much.	Sein Sportwagen **beeindruckte** sie nicht besonders.
It's dark and rainy – please drive _____!	Es ist dunkel und regnerisch – fahr bitte **vorsichtig**!
_____ well for the opera – no jeans, please!	**Zieh dich** gut für die Oper **an** – bitte keine Jeans!
He's a _____ candidate for the job.	Er ist ein **geeigneter** Kandidat für den Job.
Her main _____? She's very reliable.	Ihre Haupt**stärke**? Sie ist sehr zuverlässig.
What are your strengths and _____?	Was sind deine Stärken und **Schwächen**?
We do an _____ of all candidates.	Wir führen eine **Beurteilung** aller Kandidaten durch.
It's difficult to _____ the new situation.	Es ist schwer, die neue Lage **einzuschätzen**.
Please write on an empty _____ of paper.	Bitte schreib auf ein leeres **Blatt** Papier.
She had a sad _____ in her eyes.	Sie hatte einen traurigen **Ausdruck** in ihren Augen.
In his job in the bank he has to wear a _____.	In seinem Job in der Bank muss er **Krawatte** tragen.
I _____ back my hair when I'm cooking.	Ich **binde** mein Haar zurück, wenn ich koche.
He's eaten your chocolate? That's _____!	Er hat deine Schokolade gegessen? Das ist **frech**!

11 More about ... Networks on the Internet

Vervollständige den Text mit den passenden Wörtern aus der Box.

> application – candidates – cheeky – dangerous – impress –
> interview – join – look – opinions – profiles – reliable – suitable

When young people (1) _____ a network on the Internet, they put their names and (2) _____ online, give their (3) _____ on personal questions, or show pictures that are not (4) _____ for everyone. This can be very (5) _____ if you have sent off an (6) _____ and hope to be invited for a job (7) _____.

Companies often check the Internet to find out about their (8) _____. It won't (9) _____ your future boss to see (10) _____ pictures of you completely drunk with a stupid (11) _____ on your face – they will simply think you're not a very (12) _____ person!

2

New words ▶ pp. 41–44

As soon as we know, we'll _____ you _____ .	Sobald wir es wissen, **geben** wir Ihnen **Bescheid**.
If _____ , call him on his mobile.	Falls **nötig**, ruf ihn auf dem Handy an.
As a _____ , you sell holidays.	Als **Reisebürokauffrau** verkauft man Urlaubsreisen.
You'll find the solution – it's quite _____ .	Du wirst die Lösung finden – es ist ziemlich **einfach**.
It's all too _____ to understand.	Das ist alles zu **kompliziert**, um es zu verstehen.
There are _____ people on earth.	Es gibt **immer mehr** Menschen auf der Erde.
'Everything _____ better,' says Grandpa.	„**Früher war** alles besser", sagt Opa.
He wrote a _____ for €100.	Er zahlte mit einem **Scheck** über €100.

12 Opposites

Trage das Gegenteil der fettgedruckten Wörter in die Lücken ein.

1 stay **outdoors** / _____
2 be very **shy** / _____
3 breathe **in** / _____
4 always be **punctual** / _____
5 the **wrong** / _____ way

6 **lend** / _____ some money
7 the **death** / _____ of someone
8 my main **strength** / _____
9 be **fair** / _____ to someone
10 a **simple** / _____ story

13 Word building

Verbinde die Wörter 1–10 mit jeweils einem passenden Wort aus der Mauer. Achte dabei auf die Schreibweise (getrennt oder zusammen), und trage die deutsche Übersetzung ein.

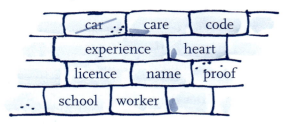

1 racing *car* _____
2 primary _____
3 work _____
4 post _____
5 first _____

6 office _____
7 water _____
8 sweet _____
9 child _____
10 driving _____

New words ▶ pp. 45–46

After the break we'll _____ our lesson.	Nach der Pause **machen** wir **weiter** mit der Stunde.
How did she _____ to the news?	Wie hat sie auf die Nachricht **reagiert**?
He waited _____, but then he left.	Er wartete **eine Weile**, aber dann ging er.
He wants to be the best – he's so _____.	Er will der Beste sein – er ist so **ehrgeizig**.
We are _____ to solve the problem.	Wir sind **entschlossen**, das Problem zu lösen.
Life is _____ with kids and a job.	Das Leben ist **stressig** mit Kindern und Beruf.
He had no idea how to _____ a business.	Er wusste nicht, wie man ein Unternehmen **leitet**.
She hasn't _____ from her trip yet.	Sie ist noch nicht von ihrer Reise **zurückgekehrt**.
Sorry, but I can't give you a _____ answer.	Ich kann dir leider keine **eindeutige** Antwort geben.
Tim has ended his _____ with Jennifer.	Tim hat seine **Beziehung** mit Jennifer beendet.
You want even more? Don't be so _____!	Du willst noch mehr? Sei nicht so **habgierig**!
I'll _____ what we've said so far.	Ich **fasse zusammen**, was wir bisher gesagt haben.

14 Two-part verbs

Vervollständige die Sätze mit einem passenden Wort von den USB-Sticks.

1 If you don't know the word, just look it _____.

2 It's warm in here. Can I take _____ my jacket?

3 I always get _____ at seven o'clock in the morning.

4 Please turn _____ the light now – you need to sleep.

5 I don't want my parents to find _____ that I have a boyfriend.

6 You have to get _____ this train at the next station.

7 It's grandpa's birthday – please put _____ your best shirt.

8 We should move _____ of this flat – the rent is too high.

9 Could you please sum _____ your main ideas again?

10 He stopped talking for a moment, but then he went _____.

11 Please hold your breath, and then breathe _____ slowly.

12 I think he's a difficult person. How do you get _____ with him?

on

off

out

up

15 Words with different meanings

Finde die passende englische Übersetzung zu den unterstrichenen deutschen Wörtern auf den Zetteln 1–6.

1)
a) Mein Rücken tut weh.
b) Komm zurück!
_____

2)
a) Ich bin gern bereit, dir das Geld zu leihen.
b) Ich bin ja so glücklich, dich zu sehen!
_____

3)
a) Ich möchte später ein Hotel leiten.
b) Kannst du 10 km in einer Stunde laufen?

4)
a) Sie hörten alle aufmerksam zu.
b) Er hat seine Arbeit sorgfältig gemacht.
_____

5)
a) Hast du schon feste Pläne fürs Wochenende?
b) Ich kann dir keine endgültige Antwort geben.
_____

6)
a) Sie sollte ihre Haare nach hinten binden.
b) Muss ich wirklich eine Krawatte tragen?

16 Crossword

Trage die Übersetzungen der deutschen Wörter ins Rätsel ein.

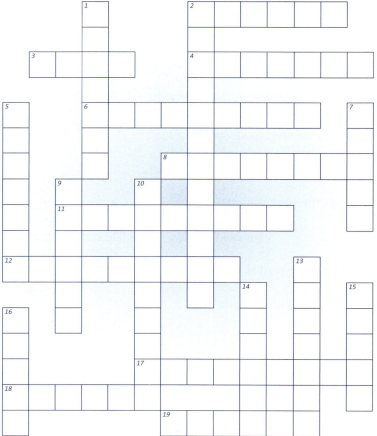

Across
- (2) zurückkehren
- (3) Formular
- (4) logisch
- (6) ehrgeizig
- (8) fortsetzen
- (11) anstrengend
- (12) dynamisch, tatkräftig
- (17) Empfang
- (18) frech, dreist
- (19) gierig

Down
- (1) Nachname
- (2) Beziehung
- (5) (einem Brief) beilegen
- (7) Blatt (Papier)
- (9) einschätzen, beurteilen
- (10) notwendig
- (13) Qualität
- (14) einfach
- (15) drucken
- (16) reagieren

17 Word groups

Ordne den vier Oberbegriffen auf den Laptops die sechs jeweils am besten passenden Wörter zu. Weitere sechs Wörter aus der Box passen zu keinem der Oberbegriffe.

advert – ambitious – assess – candidate – certificate – cheeky – chef – customer adviser – CV – dark – enclose – form – greedy – helpful – impress – mechanic – nurse – prepare – prisoner – punctual – questions – reef – reference – reliable – technology – tie – tortoise – travel agent – unconscious – vet

D5 Unit 3

New words ▶ pp. 48–50

I've no brothers or sisters – I'm an _____ .	Ich habe keine Geschwister – ich bin **Einzelkind**.
There are no hills – it's _____ for cycling.	Es gibt keine Hügel – es ist **ideal** zum Radfahren.
He _____ a doctor and help people.	Er **will** Arzt **werden** und den Menschen helfen.
Mobile phones make it easier to _____ .	Handys machen es leichter zu **kommunizieren**.
Speaking is a kind of _____ .	Sprechen ist eine Art der **Kommunikation**.
Men are _____ taller than women.	Männer sind **im Allgemeinen** größer als Frauen.
He wants to _____ smoking in the new year.	Er will im neuen Jahr **auf** das Rauchen **verzichten**.
Wake me up – my _____ is broken.	Weck mich – mein **Wecker** ist kaputt.
_____ for 6 o'clock and go to bed.	**Stell den Wecker** auf 6 Uhr und geh ins Bett.
She waited _____ , but today he didn't come.	Sie wartete **wie üblich**, aber heute kam er nicht.
She's been _____ with Tim for six weeks.	Sie **geht** seit sechs Wochen mit Tim.
I've got no mobile, but there's a _____ .	Ich habe kein Handy, aber da ist eine **Telefonzelle**.
Do you mind if I smoke? – _____ .	Stört es Sie, wenn ich rauche? – **Überhaupt nicht**.

1 Word friends

Auf jedem Plakat gibt es drei Wörter/Wortverbindungen, die direkt nach dem Verb auf dem kleinen Zettel folgen können. Unterstreiche sie.

New words ▶p. 51

He's _____ to jogging – he runs every day.   Er ist **süchtig** nach Jogging – er läuft jeden Tag.

She wore a white dress on her _____ day.   Sie trug ein weißes Kleid an ihrem **Hochzeits**tag.

Grandpa's _____ was five days after he died.   Opas **Beerdigung** war fünf Tage nachdem er starb.

Do students smoke _____ in the toilets?   Rauchen Schüler **heimlich** auf den Toiletten?

He's often lonely and feels _____.   Er ist oft einsam und fühlt sich **unerwünscht**.

Time _____ quickly during an exam.   Während einer Prüfung **vergeht** die Zeit schnell.

He _____ her _____ for Saturday night.   Er **verabredete sich** mit ihr für Samstag abend.

She _____ her boyfriend by text message!   Sie **machte** mit ihrem Freund per SMS **Schluss**!

He hasn't arrived yet – _____ he's forgotten.   Er ist noch nicht da – **vielleicht** hat er es vergessen.

2 Crossword

Trage die Übersetzungen der deutschen Wörter ins Rätsel ein.

Across
- (3) schütteln, zittern
- (4) Postleitzahl
- (6) zuverlässig
- (9) Koch
- (10) unerwünscht, ungewollt
- (13) (Hotel etc.) leiten
- (15) kommunizieren
- (19) vielleicht
- (20) passend, geeignet
- (21) Beerdigung

Down
- (1) heimlich
- (2) Bewerbung
- (3) ähnlich
- (5) Hochzeit
- (7) pünktlich
- (8) Zukunft
- (11) mit jm. Schluss machen
- (12) allgemein
- (14) Entscheidung
- (16) ehrlich
- (17) reparieren
- (18) Fähigkeit, Fertigkeit

New words ▶ p. 52

I am writing _____ your letter of 8 May.	**In Beantwortung** Ihres Briefes vom 8. Mai …
I'm _____ at the moment – I'll call you later.	Ich bin gerade **beschäftigt** – ich rufe dich später an.
Tell her _____, not on the phone.	Sag es ihr **persönlich**, nicht am Telefon.
I _____ when someone is late.	Ich **ärgere mich**, wenn jemand zu spät kommt.
Should we _____ mobiles from school?	Sollten wir Handys in der Schule **verbieten**?
Smoking isn't allowed in _____ buildings.	Rauchen ist in **öffentlichen** Gebäuden nicht erlaubt.
The list isn't _____ – one thing's missing.	Die Liste ist nicht **vollständig** – eine Sache fehlt.
Granny does breakdance? That's _____!	Oma macht Breakdance? Das ist **albern**!

3 The best word

Finde das Wort A, B, C oder D, das am besten in die Lücke passt.

A	by	B	away
C	off	D	over

1 A whole hour went _____ before a bus came.

A	assessed	B	dressed
C	impressed	D	pressed

2 They were very _____ by the candidate's strengths.

A	one	B	once
C	only	D	own

3 A(n) _____ child has no brothers or sisters.

A	dump	B	tie
C	serve	D	ban

4 They should _____ drinking from stadiums.

A	ridiculous	B	annoyed
C	addicted	D	complete

5 That pink and green hat looks _____.

A	finished	B	dumped
C	ended	D	stopped

6 She _____ her boyfriend after only three days!

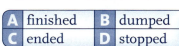

4 Odd word out

*Ein Wort passt nicht.
Finde und unterstreiche es.*

1 stupid – silly – busy – ridiculous

2 best – ideal – perfect – public

3 go by – put on – wear – dress

4 complete – full – whole – greedy

5 hat – sheet – jacket – tie

6 wedding – funeral – birthday – communication

7 determined – unwanted – confident – energetic

8 dump – speak – talk – communicate

9 generally – secretly – usually – normally

10 bush – desert – college – outback

New words ▶ p. 53

If you don't hurry up, you'll _____ the train.	Wenn du dich nicht beeilst, **verpasst** du den Zug.
He _____ the file under 'mail.doc'.	Er **speicherte** die Datei unter „mail.doc".
Mr Smith? _____, I'll see if he's there.	Herr Smith? **Augenblick**, ich schaue, ob er da ist.
The _____ is €1.20 to the pound.	Der **Wechselkurs** ist €1,20 für ein Pfund.
I'll just get some _____ from the bank.	Ich gehe nur etwas **Bargeld** von der Bank holen.
You can pay cash or by _____.	Du kannst bar oder mit **Kreditkarte** bezahlen.
She took a £20 _____ out of her purse.	Sie nahm einen £20-**Schein** aus ihrer Geldbörse.
They _____ that website – it was horrible!	Die Webseite wurde **gesperrt** – sie war grauenhaft!
_____ your password and click 'OK'.	**Gib** dein Passwort **ein** und klicke auf „OK".
Here's your change and your _____.	Hier ist das Wechselgeld und Ihre **Quittung**.

5 Words with different meanings

Finde die passende englische Übersetzung zu den unterstrichenen deutschen Wörtern auf den Zetteln 1–6.

1)
a) Ich muss die Nummer noch <u>abspeichern</u>.
b) Ich bin sicher, sie werden uns <u>retten</u>.

2)
a) Der Tennisplatz ist <u>geschlossen</u>.
b) Er arbeitet am <u>Gericht</u>.

3)
a) Wir durften das Gebäude nicht <u>betreten</u>.
b) Du musst zuerst die PIN <u>eingeben</u>.

4)
a) Ich habe nur einen 100-Euro-<u>Schein</u>.
b) Hast du nicht die <u>Notiz</u> gelesen?

5)
a) Ich <u>vermisse</u> meine Freundin.
b) Beeil dich, sonst <u>verpassen</u> wir den Bus.

6)
a) Was <u>bedeutet</u> das?
b) Was <u>meinst</u> du damit?

6 Making new words

Bilde aus den Buchstaben des Wortes so viele neue Wörter wie möglich. Wenn du fünf Wörter findest: nicht schlecht. Zehn Wörter: sehr gut. 15 oder mehr Wörter: absolute Spitze!

went, and,

unwanted

28 **3**

New words ▸ p. 54

He annoys people – he's a real _____.	Er ärgert die Leute – er ist ein echter **Unruhestifter**.
Bullying is anti-social _____.	Andere zu tyrannisieren ist unsoziales **Verhalten**.
She _____ as if nothing had happened.	Sie **verhielt** sich so, als ob nichts passiert wäre.
You have to do it! It's an _____ from the boss.	Du musst es tun! Es ist eine **Anordnung** vom Chef.
She sent him to his room as a _____.	Als **Strafe** schickte sie ihn auf sein Zimmer.
Do you _____ your kids for bad behaviour?	**Bestrafst** du deine Kinder für schlechtes Verhalten?
I'll _____ the poster _____ in my room.	Ich **hänge** das Poster in meinem Zimmer **auf**.
Use glue to _____ the photos into the album.	Nimm Klebstoff, um die Fotos ins Album zu **kleben**.
Graffiti is sometimes even _____ on trains.	Graffiti wird manchmal sogar auf Züge **gesprüht**.
He was caught when he was _____.	Er wurde erwischt, als er **Ladendiebstahl beging**.
Stealing things from a shop is _____.	In einem Geschäft zu klauen ist **Ladendiebstahl**.
The terrorist _____ us with a gun.	Der Terrorist **bedrohte** uns mit einem Gewehr.
Look! Someone has _____ my car!	Schau! Jemand hat mein Auto **mutwillig beschädigt**!
Is graffiti art or _____?	Ist Graffiti Kunst oder **Vandalismus**?
I can't serve two people _____.	Ich kann nicht zwei Leute **gleichzeitig** bedienen!

7 Word families

a) Finde die passenden Nomen zu den angegebenen Verben.

1 assess – _____

2 behave – _____

3 punish – _____

4 revise – _____

5 vandalize – _____

6 succeed – _____

7 advise – _____

8 save – _____

9 imagine – _____

b) Vervollständige die Sätze mit der korrekten Form eines Verbs oder Nomens aus a).

1 You have no idea? Well, use your _____!

2 The band's new album is a huge _____.

3 Oh dear! I forgot to _____ the file before the program crashed.

4 He didn't _____ in finding a new job.

5 If you don't _____ yourself, you'll have to go to your room.

New words ▸ pp. 55–58 (part 1)

Her death was _____ news for us.	Ihr Tod war eine **schockierende** Nachricht für uns.
Soldiers must first learn strict _____.	Soldaten müssen zuerst strenge **Disziplin** lernen.
I was in Rome, Paris and _____ London.	Ich war in Rom, Paris, und **zuletzt** in London.
It was a _____ time when he had no job.	Die Zeit war **sorgenvoll**, als er keinen Job hatte.
The picture isn't beautiful at all – it's _____!	Das Bild ist überhaupt nicht schön – es ist **hässlich**!
People should help in their local _____.	Die Leute sollten in ihrer Orts**gemeinde** helfen.
The water is from a clean mountain _____.	Das Wasser ist aus seiner sauberen Berg**quelle**.
Put your _____ in the bin!	Tu deinen **Müll** in die Tonne!
When I shop I never ask for a _____ bag.	Beim Einkaufen frage ich nie nach einer **Plastik**tüte.
I like Jenny. She's _____ a nice girl!	Ich mag Jenny. Sie ist **so** ein nettes Mädchen!

8 Word search: Teens in trouble

Finde 16 Begriffe aus dem Wortfeld
„Randalierer/Unruhestifter". (↓ →)
Übersetze sie ins Deutsche.

Z	P	U	N	I	S	H	H	D	Y	L	S
T	R	O	U	B	L	E	W	D	Q	R	B
X	V	R	B	A	N	T	Q	V	Q	U	E
D	T	T	H	R	E	A	T	E	N	L	H
V	A	N	D	A	L	I	S	M	M	E	A
P	P	G	I	X	C	R	I	M	E	S	V
A	R	D	S	G	R	A	F	F	I	T	I
J	I	R	C	F	L	E	R	D	P	A	O
E	S	U	I	B	S	B	J	Z	I	N	U
E	O	G	P	C	L	G	V	K	S	A	R
U	N	S	L	S	H	O	P	L	I	F	T
F	P	V	I	O	L	E	N	C	E	Y	F
Z	M	S	N	U	W	F	I	G	H	T	B
N	J	A	E	B	U	L	L	Y	I	N	G

behaviour – Verhalten

_____

_____

_____

_____

_____

_____

_____

_____

_____

_____

_____

_____

_____

_____

_____

30 **3**

New words ▶ pp. 58 (part 2) – 60

It's _____ that I couldn't meet her.   Es ist **ein Jammer**, dass ich sie nicht treffen konnte.

A _____ swims with four legs.   Eine **Wasserschildkröte** schwimmt mit vier Beinen.

Horses _____ eat grass.   Pferde fressen **hauptsächlich** Gras.

The story of Jesus Christ is in the _____.   Die Geschichte von Jesus Christus ist in der **Bibel**.

They _____ a meeting about the project.   Sie **hielten** eine Besprechung über das Projekt **ab**.

This ticket machine only takes _____.   Dieser Fahrkartenautomat nimmt nur **Münzen**.

She put the $10 _____ into her purse.   Sie steckte den $10-**Schein** in ihre Geldbörse.

Is fresh fruit better than _____ fruit?   Ist frisches Obst besser als Obst **in Dosen**?

You can buy cola in _____ or bottles.   Man kann Cola in **Dosen** oder Flaschen kaufen.

You should _____ potatoes cool and dark.   Man sollte Kartoffeln kühl und dunkel **lagern**.

He stayed _____ in London after the show.   Er blieb **über Nacht** in London nach der Show.

Don't drink any _____ when you drive.   Trink keinen **Alkohol**, wenn du fährst.

9 Pronunciation

Ordne die Wörter der richtigen Aussprachegruppe zu, je nachdem, wie der unterstrichene Vokal ausgesprochen wird.

əʊ	ɒ	ɔː	ə
enclose			

college, complete, hold, more, customer, instructor, shoplift, police, mostly, alcohol, order, block, organized, overnight, postcode, contact, store, continue, solve, note, form, enclose, normal, community

New words ▶ p. 62

When I'm embarrassed, I _____.	Wenn mir etwas peinlich ist, **werde** ich **rot**.
He called her, but her phone was _____.	Er rief sie an, aber es war **besetzt**.
I believe him – he never _____ to me.	Ich glaube ihm – er **lügt** mich nie an.
He _____ his new expensive watch.	Er **prahlte** mit seiner neuen, teuren Uhr.
I knew it was just a trick. _____!	Ich wusste, es war nur ein Trick. **Netter Versuch!**
He's angry. When I called him, he just _____.	Er ist sauer. Als ich ihn anrief, **legte** er einfach **auf**.

10 Words with a similar meaning

Finde Wörter, die das Gleiche bedeuten wie die fettgedruckten Wörter.
Trage sie ein und schreibe die deutsche Übersetzung auf.

1 My father has always been a **supporter** / _fan_ of ManU.   _Anhänger/in_

2 Are you coming? – **Wait a minute** / _____. I'm not ready yet.   _____

3 Cows eat **mostly** / _____ grass.   _____

4 I **fully** / _____ understand why you're angry.   _____

5 He's not here. **Maybe** / _____ he's gone home.   _____

6 I think I look **silly** / _____ in this pink shirt.   _____

7 He was late, so he **didn't get** / _____ the bus.   _____

8 I want to **glue** / _____ the photos into an album.   _____

11 Lost words

Ergänze die Sätze mit der jeweils korrekten Präposition.
Bei einem der Sätze bleibt die Lücke leer.

1 Sorry, but I can only do one thing _____ a time.

2 You can pay cash or _____ credit card.

3 When he said 'I love you', she went _____ red.

4 Sandra really has no interest _____ football.

5 Last week I got quite annoyed _____ her.

6 At last we were able to talk face _____ face.

7 They gave him a cheque _____ 100 euros.

8 _____ Monday his mobile was busy all day!

New words ▶ pp. 63–64

Granny lives in an _____.	Oma lebt im **Altenheim**.
What have I done to _____ this?	Was habe ich getan, dass ich das **verdiene**?
There was a loud _____ on my door.	Es **klopfte** laut an meiner Tür.
Always _____ at her door before you enter.	**Klopfe** immer an ihrer Tür, bevor du eintrittst.
In church you often say a lot of _____.	In der Kirche spricht man oft viele **Gebete**.
Some people go down on their knees to _____.	Manche Leute gehen auf die Knie um zu **beten**.
_____ 999 to call the police.	**Wähle** die 999, um die Polizei anzurufen.
I don't want to see you – _____ me _____ !	Ich will dich nicht sehen – **lass** mich **in Ruhe**!
After the rain the path was very _____.	Nach dem Regen war der Pfad sehr **matschig**.
Wear boots if you walk through _____.	Trage Stiefel, wenn du durch **Matsch** gehst.
I heard loud _____ coming up the stairs.	Ich hörte laute **Schritte** die Treppe hochkommen.
The film is exciting – really _____ !	Der Film ist spannend – wirklich **aufregend**!

12 Definitions

Vervollständige die Definitionen mit Wörtern aus dem linken Display.
Trage die richtige Lösung aus dem anderen Display in die rechte Spalte ein.

crime door earth hand paper place shoes shop things water

knock mud receipt shoplifting spring

1 when you hit a _*door*_ with your _____ before you open it _____

2 a _____ where _____ comes out of the ground _____

3 wet _____ that is soft and sticks to your _____ _____

4 a piece of _____ that shows the _____ you have paid for _____

5 the _____ of stealing something from a _____ _____

13 Verb forms

Ergänze die Tabelle der unregelmäßigen Verben.

1	get	got	got
2	shake		
3		spoke	
4			gone
5	bleed		
6			set
7		ran	

8			left
9		gave	
10			hung
11		held	
12	make		
13		stuck	
14			lent

14 Word building

Verbinde die Wörter 1 – 8 mit jeweils einem passenden Wort aus der Mauer. Achte dabei auf die Schreibweise (getrennt oder zusammen), und trage die deutsche Übersetzung ein.

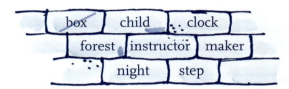

1 phone *box* _____
2 foot _____ _____
3 alarm _____ _____
4 only _____ _____
5 rain _____ _____
6 trouble _____ _____
7 over _____ _____
8 driving _____ _____

15 Spot the mistakes

In jedem Satz sind zwei Fehler.
Unterstreiche und korrigiere sie.

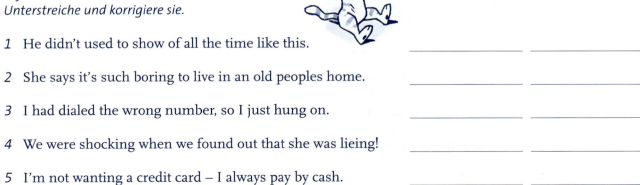

1 He didn't used to show of all the time like this. _____ _____

2 She says it's such boring to live in an old peoples home. _____ _____

3 I had dialed the wrong number, so I just hung on. _____ _____

4 We were shocking when we found out that she was lieing! _____ _____

5 I'm not wanting a credit card – I always pay by cash. _____ _____

D5 Unit 4

34

New words ▸ pp. 74–75

It's a fan website, not the _____ one.	Es ist eine Fan-Webseite, nicht die **offizielle**.
_____ is destroying our world.	**Umweltverschmutzung** zerstört unsere Welt.
The lake is so _____ that there are no fish.	Der See ist so **verseucht**, dass es keine Fische gibt.
The _____ between rich and poor is huge.	Der **Gegensatz** zwischen arm und reich ist riesig.
My bank gives me good _____ advice.	Meine Bank gibt mir gute **finanzielle** Ratschläge.
He wants €200 – that's a _____ of the €600.	Er will €200 – das ist **ein Drittel** der €600.
_____ is high – there are no jobs.	Die **Arbeitslosigkeit** ist hoch – es gibt keine Jobs.
Wimbledon is a _____ of London.	Wimbledon ist ein **Vorort** von London.
He uses _____, not the car.	Er nimmt **öffentliche Verkehrsmittel**, nicht das Auto.

1 Words with a similar meaning

Finde Wörter, die das Gleiche bedeuten wie die fettgedruckten Wörter.
Trage sie ein und schreibe die deutsche Übersetzung auf.

1 She's really **afraid** / _scared_ of spiders.   _sich fürchten_

2 The air conditioning cost **almost** / _____ £2,000!   _____

3 There's not enough **room** / _____ in the garage for the bike.   _____

4 We hoped he would **come back** / _____, but he never did.   _____

5 About **33.3 per cent** / _____ of the people are poor.   _____

6 The train was so **full** / _____ – I could hardly get on.   _____

7 Tomorrow we will **go on** / _____ with our lesson.   _____

8 I often go to India – I was in Mumbai **not long ago** / _____.   _____

9 Don't forget to **enclose** / _____ your CV.   _____

10 It's best to go by **bus, tram or tube** / _____.   _____

11 You can't swim in this river – it's too **dirty** / _____.   _____

12 My computer is OK, but I need a new **screen** / _____.   _____

New words ▶ p. 76

It's a good film – all the reviews are _____.	Der Film ist gut – alle Kritiken sind **positiv**.
It's not so bad – you're simply too _____.	Es ist nicht so schlecht – du bist einfach zu **negativ**.
Ask the shop assistant – she's very _____.	Frag die Verkäuferin – sie ist sehr **hilfsbereit**.
This house is _____ of the 18th century.	Dieses Haus ist **typisch** für das 18. Jahrhundert.
Some families _____ $1 a day!	Manche Familien **leben von** $1 am Tag!
Canadian forests are _____ in autumn.	Kanadische Wälder sind **farbenprächtig** im Herbst.
If you are _____, you should stay in bed.	Wenn du **krank** bist, solltest du im Bett bleiben.

2 Lost words

Ergänze die Sätze mit der jeweils korrekten Präposition.

1 There were too many people _____ the train.
2 The bus was crowded _____ people.
3 Tom will be late again – that's typical _____ him!
4 The temperature has risen _____ ten per cent.
5 Unemployment is very high _____ the moment.
6 We live _____ a suburb of Manchester.
7 Oh please, leave me alone _____ a while!
8 Hold on _____ my arm, Granny – I'll help you to walk.

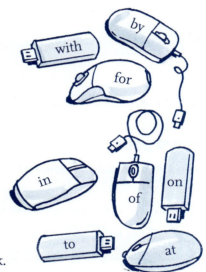

3 The best word

Finde das Wort A, B, C oder D, das am besten in die Lücke passt.

A official	B financial
C typical	D final

1 My bank gives me good _____ advice.

A colourful	B stressful
C beautiful	D helpful

2 Their advice is always _____.

A contrast	B control
C context	D concert

3 The _____ between rich and poor is huge.

A players	B papers
C prayers	D painters

4 They say a lot of _____ in church.

A lied	B laid
C lay	D lain

5 Don't believe him – he _____ to you!

4

New words ▸ p. 77

The cat _____ to its new home.	Die Katze **gewöhnte** sich an ihr neues Zuhause.
Ask Tom – he's _____ with the program.	Frag Tom – er **kennt sich aus** mit dem Programm.
About 2200 people were _____ the Titanic.	Etwa 2200 Menschen waren **an Bord** der Titanic.
They had to discuss every _____ little detail.	Sie mussten jedes **winzig** kleine Detail diskutieren.
He wanted to leave, but she _____ to him.	Er wollte gehen, aber sie **hielt sich** an ihm **fest**.
She bought a golden _____ for the picture.	Sie kaufte einen goldenen **Rahmen** für das Bild.
He _____ out of the window and almost fell.	Er **lehnte sich** aus dem Fenster und fiel dabei fast.
There weren't many _____ on board.	Es waren nicht viele **Passagiere** an Bord.
I can't wear these jeans – they're too _____.	Ich kann diese Jeans nicht tragen – sie ist zu **eng**.
_____ believe we will be born again.	**Hindus** glauben, dass wir wiedergeboren werden.
A lot of _____ don't eat during Ramadan.	Viele **Muslime** essen nichts während des Ramadan.
_____ believe in Jesus Christ.	**Christen** glauben an Jesus Christus.

4 Word pairs

Welche Wörter passen zusammen?

1) adjust to
2) air
3) become
4) canned
5) Christian
6) crowded
7) door
8) polluted
9) secret
10) tight

belief
the dark
frame
fruit
jeans
lover
pollution
river
tram
wet

New words ▸ p. 78

In Africa lots of people live in _____.	In Afrika leben viele Menschen in **Armut**.
_____ means you have no home.	**Obdachlosigkeit** heißt, dass man kein Zuhause hat.
I find that museum really _____.	Ich finde das Museum wirklich **faszinierend**.
That dress looks great – very _____!	Das Kleid sieht toll aus – sehr **schick**!
His job's very _____ – he's a movie star.	Sein Beruf ist sehr **glamourös** – er ist ein Filmstar.

5 Definitions

Vervollständige die Definitionen mit Wörtern aus dem Laptop-Monitor.
Trage die richtige Lösung von den USB-Sticks in die rechte Spalte ein.

Laptop monitor words: area, centre, difference, factory, job, number, person, things, train, water

USB sticks: contrast, passenger, suburb, pollution, unemployment

1 when, for example, a _____ makes the air, _____ or earth dirty   _____

2 a _____ between two _____ that you can see clearly   _____

3 an _____ where people live that is outside the _____ of a city   _____

4 the fact that a _____ of people have no _____   _____

5 a _____ who is travelling in a bus, _____, plane or ship   _____

6 Odd word out

Ein Wort passt nicht.
Finde und unterstreiche es.

1 Hindu – Indian – Muslim – Christian

2 thrilling – fascinating – exciting – worrying

3 fashionable – official – trendy – modern

4 poverty – unemployment – ink – homelessness

5 railway – highway – road – street

6 sick – tiny – small – little

7 cash – coin – note – frame

8 trash – plant – pollution – rubbish

4

New words ▸ p. 79

I won't join you – _____. Ich komme nicht mit – **ich fühle mich nicht wohl**.

She's ill – a cold, or perhaps the _____. Sie ist krank – Erkältung, oder vielleicht die **Grippe**.

Whenever I run, I get _____ in my knee. Wenn ich laufe, bekomme ich **Schmerzen** im Knie.

A computer _____ destroyed the program. Ein Computer**virus** hat das Programm zerstört.

The doctor gave her some _____ for her skin. Der Arzt gab ihr eine **Salbe** für die Haut.

He studied _____ – now he's a doctor. Er hat **Medizin** studiert – jetzt ist er Arzt.

Take one _____ before meals with some water. Nimm eine **Pille** vor dem Essen mit etwas Wasser.

You need a _____ to buy these pills. Man braucht ein **Rezept**, um die Pillen zu kaufen.

The hospital has beds for 120 _____. Das Krankenhaus hat Betten für 120 **Patienten**.

7 Crossword

Trage die Übersetzungen der deutschen Wörter ins Rätsel ein.

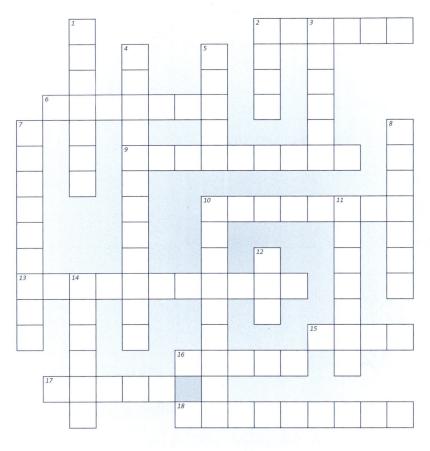

Across
- (2) Gebet
- (6) (zu Recht) verdienen
- (9) Gemeinde
- (10) Schritt
- (13) modisch, schick
- (15) Schmerz
- (16) dicht, eng
- (17) Rahmen / Gestell
- (18) glamourös

Down
- (1) Armut
- (2) Tablette
- (3) sich anpassen, gewöhnen
- (4) Rezept (für Medikamente)
- (5) Salbe
- (7) farbenfroh, farbig
- (8) hilfsbereit / nützlich
- (10) finanziell
- (11) typisch
- (12) Grippe
- (14) Vorort

New words ▶ p. 80

From the tower you have an _____ view.	Vom Turm hat man eine **beeindruckende** Aussicht.
There was no _____ water in the slum.	Im Slum gab es kein **fließendes** Wasser.
The slum people live and sleep in _____ .	Die Slumbewohner wohnen und schlafen in **Hütten**.
Gold is a valuable _____ .	Gold ist ein wertvolles **Metall**.
In _____ soccer you only have five players.	Beim **Hallen**fussball hat man nur fünf Spieler.
The _____ swimming pool closes in winter.	Das **Frei**bad schließt im Winter.
The _____ of the movie fights against crime.	Der **Held** des Films kämpft gegen das Verbrechen.
A world trip is an _____ experience.	Eine Weltreise ist ein **unvergessliches** Erlebnis.

8 Opposites

Trage das Gegenteil der fettgedruckten Wörter in die Lücken ein.

1 an **indoor** / _____ swimming pool

2 a **huge** / _____ difference

3 **agree** / _____ with somebody

4 a **quiet** / _____ street

5 live in **the centre** / a _____ of a city

6 look from the **outside** / _____

7 a **wanted** / an _____ child

8 a **positive** / _____ experience

9 a **crowded** / an _____ room

10 wear **fashionable** / _____ clothes

11 **beautiful** / _____ people

12 do **well** / _____ in a test

13 be **single** / _____

14 suddenly **appear** / _____

15 a **true** / _____ story

16 **buy** / _____ a car

17 a **strong** / _____ man

18 the **best** / _____ novel

19 **healthy** / _____ food

20 a **clean** / _____ river

9 The fourth word

Welches Wort fehlt hier?

1 land – tortoise   water – _____

2 BE – rubbish   AE – _____

3 two – a half   three – _____

4 car – mechanic   computer – _____

5 crowd – crowded   can – _____

6 teacher – student   doctor – _____

7 8-year-old – child   30-year-old – _____

8 credit card – plastic   coin – _____

4

New words ▶p. 81

Oh, it's you! I didn't _____ you at first.   Ach, du bist es! Ich habe dich zuerst nicht **erkannt**.

In a democracy there is _____ of speech.   In einer Demokratie gibt es Rede**freiheit**.

Don't be shy – have more _____!   Sei nicht schüchtern – hab mehr **Selbstvertrauen**!

I like the _____ of your clothes – very trendy!   Ich mag den **Stil** deiner Kleider – sehr modisch!

Do you like _____ or tight jeans?   Magst du **weite** oder enge Jeans?

He pulled his _____ over his eyes.   Er zog seinen **Schlapphut** über die Augen.

East Germany had a different _____ system.   Die DDR hatte ein anderes **politisches** System.

A mayor is active in local _____.   Ein Bürgermeister ist in der Lokal**politik** tätig.

Hurry up! The train is _____ leave.   Beeil dich! Der Zug ist **im Begriff** abzufahren!

The star took the pen and gave her an _____.   Der Star nahm den Stift und gab ihr ein **Autogramm**.

10 Verb forms

Ergänze die Tabelle der unregelmäßigen Verben.

1	take	took	taken
2		hurt	
3	catch		
4		held	
5	build		
6			drunk

7			hung
8	let		
9		stood	
10			risen
11	teach		
12		shot	

11 Spot the mistakes

In jedem Satz sind zwei Fehler. Unterstreiche und korrigiere sie.

1 The two heros of the film fight for peoples freedom.

2 When I recognized the star, I've asked her for an autogram.

3 The doctor gave me a receipt for some skin creme.

4 Mumbai is a huge, colourfull city – it's really impressing!

5 He live in a slum with no electricity or runing water.

6 How many woman are really interesting in football?

New words ▶p. 83

The pub has a _____ room for smokers.	Die Kneipe hat einen **separaten** Raucherraum.
She wanted to leave, but he _____ her to stay.	Sie wollte gehen, aber er **zwang** sie zu bleiben.
FIFA is the International Football _____.	FIFA ist der Internationale Fußball**verband**.
_____ between the countries are good.	Die **Beziehungen** zwischen den Ländern sind gut.

12 Two-part verbs

Vervollständige die Sätze mit einem passenden Wort von den USB-Sticks.

1 Don't lean _____ of the window – it's dangerous!
2 Hold _____ to my arm, Granny – I'll help you to walk.
3 You'll have to give _____ alcohol if you want to get fit.
4 Alan showed _____ his expensive new watch.
5 Can you really live _____ one dollar a day?
6 Don't worry – things will work _____ in the end.
7 He tore _____ a piece of paper to write down her number.
8 Sorry, no tickets anymore. The concert is sold _____.
9 Now hang _____ a second – that can't be true!
10 What a nice poster – I'll stick it _____ in my room.

13 Making new words

Bilde aus den Buchstaben des Wortes so viele neue Wörter wie möglich.
30 Wörter solltest du leicht finden, aber wer findet über 50?

ear, listen,

relations

42 **4**

New words ▸pp. 84–85

Every day, animals have to fight for _____ .   Jeden Tag müssen Tiere ums **Überleben** kämpfen.

Does the _____ contain the right tools?   Sind die richtigen Werkzeuge bei der **Ausrüstung**?

I'll _____ a table at the Chinese restaurant.   Ich **reserviere** einen Tisch im Chinarestaurant.

You have to show your _____ at the border.   An der Grenze musst du deinen **Reisepass** zeigen.

Is there _____ ? A hotel?   Gibt es einen **Platz zum Übernachten**? Ein Hotel?

We slept in the hostel's large _____ .   Wir schliefen im großen **Schlafsaal** der Herberge.

A _____ or two single rooms?   Ein **Doppelzimmer** oder zwei Einzelzimmer?

The _____ is below the ground floor.   Das **Kellergeschoss** ist unter dem Erdgeschoss.

I didn't know that. You _____ me!   Ich wusste es nicht. Du **hättest** es mir **sagen sollen**!

I'm hungry – do you _____ going for a meal?   Ich habe Hunger – **hast du Lust**, essen zu gehen?

There's a café _____ of the tower.   **Oben auf** dem Turm gibt es ein Café.

He had to _____ for an hour to get in.   Er musste eine Stunde **anstehen**, um reinzukommen.

14 Words with different meanings

Finde auf der Liste (Seestern-Magnet) ein passendes Wort zu den beiden Sätzen/Satzteilen auf den Zetteln 1 – 9.
Trage es dort ein und unterstreiche die beiden deutschen Entsprechungen.

1)
a) Ich möchte ein Doppelzimmer <u>reservieren</u>.

b) Es ist ein spannendes <u>Buch</u>.

book

2)
a) Ich freue mich schon auf den Frühling.

b) In dem Dorf gibt es eine Quelle.

3)
a) Können Sie mir bitte helfen?

b) Hier, nimm noch eine Dose Cola.

4)
a) Er kann nicht auf dem Rücken liegen.

b) Du solltest nicht lügen.

5)
a) Diese Jeans ist sehr eng.

b) Halt mich fest!

6)
a) Können wir bitte bestellen?

b) Es ist ein Befehl vom Chef.

7)
a) Der Arzt gab ihr eine Salbe.

b) Möchtest du Sahne zum Kuchen?

8)
a) Schreib das an die Tafel.

b) Es sind alle Passagiere an Bord.

9)
a) Können wir bitte die Rechnung haben?

b) Ich habe noch einen 10-Dollar-Schein.

bill
board
~~book~~
can
cream
lie
order
spring
tight

New words ▸p. 86

Can I make a phone call? – Yes, _____ ! Darf ich mal telefonieren? – Aber **sicherlich**!

Room 52 wants a _____ at 6 am. Zimmer 52 möchte einen **Weckanruf** um 6 Uhr.

We wish you a _____ flight. Wir wünschen Ihnen einen **angenehmen** Flug.

Did you have a pleasant _____ in our hotel? Hatten Sie einen angenehmen **Aufenthalt** im Hotel?

There are no rooms left – we're _____ . Es gibt keine Zimmer mehr – wir sind **ausgebucht**.

You can now _____ for your flight. Sie können sich jetzt für Ihren Flug **einchecken**.

Is there an Internet _____ in the room? Gibt es eine Internet**verbindung** auf dem Zimmer?

A tunnel _____ England with France. Ein Tunnel **verbindet** England mit Frankreich.

In English pubs you pay _____ – not later. In englischen Pubs zahlt man **sofort** – nicht später.

Please _____ after the beep. Bitte **hinterlassen Sie eine Nachricht** nach dem Ton.

He's not in. Can I _____ ? Er ist nicht da. Kann ich **ihm etwas ausrichten**?

15 Word families

a) Finde die passenden Adjektive zu den angegebenen Nomen.

1 friendliness – _____

2 confidence – _____

3 pollution – _____

4 strength – _____

5 politics – _____

6 pain – _____

7 nature – _____

8 mud – _____

9 racist – _____

10 art – _____

11 fashion – _____

12 weakness – _____

13 freedom – _____

14 poverty – _____

15 poison – _____

b) Vervollständige die Sätze mit der korrekten Form eines Adjektivs oder Nomens aus a).

1 Even in rich countries too many people live in _____ .

2 Be careful! This snake is _____ !

3 Sara is much too shy – she just has no _____ .

4 Fish can't survive in this river – it's too _____ .

5 The field was really _____ after three days of rain.

6 I love _____ films about wild animals.

7 He was in prison for six years, but now he's _____ .

8 This shop has the most trendy and _____ clothes in town.

New words ▶pp. 87–88

Do you wear _____ and tie in your job?	Trägst du **Anzug** und Krawatte in deinem Job?
She practised her _____ in front of a mirror.	Sie übte ihren **Vortrag** vor dem Spiegel.
A student _____ on Berlin.	Ein Schüler **hielt einen Vortrag** über Berlin.
Today the teacher _____ a new topic.	Heute **hat** der Lehrer ein neues Thema **eingeführt**.
The lights created amazing _____ effects.	Die Lichter erzeugten erstaunliche **optische** Effekte.
What _____ is the shirt made of? – Cotton.	Aus welchem **Material** ist das Hemd? – Baumwolle.
You need at least _____ computer skills.	Du brauchst zumindest Computer-**Grund**kenntnisse.
The smell _____ her _____ to the gas.	Der Geruch **machte** sie auf das Gas **aufmerksam**.
Please _____ to contact us at any time.	Sie **können** uns **gerne** jederzeit kontaktieren.
We saw a _____-show about Australia.	Wir sahen eine **Dia**show über Australien.

16 Word groups

*Ordne den drei Oberbegriffen auf den Laptops jeweils sechs passende Wörter zu.
Weitere sechs Wörter aus der Box passen zu keinem der Oberbegriffe.*

audience – autograph – baggy – (to) book – breakfast – chart – cream – dormitory – double room – freedom – glamorous – medicine – overnight – pain – patient – pill – politics – prescription – (to) present – reception – shack – slide – talk – visual

4

17 Word search: Big city life

Finde 20 Begriffe aus dem Wortfeld „Leben in der Großstadt". (↓ →)
Übersetze sie ins Deutsche.

B	T	M	G	W	T	R	A	F	F	I	C	V	R	Z	V	Z	L	T	Q	Y	N	R	J
P	Q	G	A	H	R	V	O	S	E	T	P	O	L	L	U	T	I	O	N	W	R	T	I
A	I	R	P	O	R	T	V	D	X	K	J	Y	L	O	Y	T	R	U	T	Q	B	L	S
V	V	A	V	T	M	R	T	A	H	T	Y	P	S	K	Y	S	C	R	A	P	E	R	M
E	C	F	T	E	U	A	E	G	S	H	O	P	S	Q	U	T	Z	I	T	S	U	R	H
M	S	F	Q	L	I	M	A	R	K	E	T	F	W	V	Q	A	E	S	L	U	M	J	U
E	K	I	Z	M	D	Y	P	J	I	A	M	C	G	G	Q	T	L	T	W	B	O	D	U
N	S	T	R	E	E	T	T	K	S	T	A	D	I	U	M	I	Y	S	Q	U	A	R	E
T	Z	I	Q	K	E	N	A	I	T	R	Y	S	M	Y	X	O	Y	C	Z	R	E	K	D
N	Q	J	Z	X	Q	O	U	N	D	E	R	G	R	O	U	N	D	B	V	B	U	S	S

airport – Flughafen

_____   _____   _____

_____   _____   _____

_____   _____   _____

_____   _____   _____

_____   _____   _____

_____   _____   _____

18 Word stress

Unterstreiche bei allen Wörtern die Silbe, die betont werden muss.

autograph	candidate	contrast	credit card
discipline	double room	fashionable	financial
glamorous	material	medicine	metal
Muslim	official	passenger	patient
politics	popular	separate	social
tourist	transport	vandalism	visual

D6 Unit 1

New words ▸ p. 6

She's so _____ – I liked her immediately.	Sie ist so **charmant** – ich mochte sie sofort.
He's tall, dark and very _____.	Er ist groß, dunkel und sehr **gut aussehend**.
She loved Tim, but he didn't _____ her.	Sie liebte Tim, aber er **stand** nicht auf sie.
It's _____ to think you're something better.	Es ist **arrogant**, sich für etwas Besseres zu halten.
She always stayed _____ to her boss.	Sie blieb ihrem Chef gegenüber immer **loyal**.
He tells everyone what to do – he's so _____!	Er sagt jedem, was er tun soll – er ist so **herrisch**!
I find her quite _____ in that beautiful dress.	Ich finde sie sehr **attraktiv** in dem schönen Kleid.
She says her big nose makes her _____.	Sie sagt, ihre große Nase mache sie **unattraktiv**.
A beard and glasses change your _____.	Bart und Brille verändern dein **Aussehen**.
Her hair was long, blond and _____.	Ihr Haar war lang, blond und **lockig**.
His hair was curly, not _____.	Sein Haar war lockig, nicht **glatt**.
He never laughs – he has no _____.	Er lacht nie – er hat keinen **Sinn für Humor**.
Do you like nuts? – Only _____, without salt.	Magst du Nüsse? – Nur **Erdnüsse**, ohne Salz.
Spain is always sunny, _____ Ireland.	Spanien ist immer sonnig, **im Gegensatz zu** Irland.

1 The best word

Finde das Wort A, B, C oder D, das am besten in die Lücke passt.

A	find	B	notice
C	nod	D	attract

1 Did you _____ her hair? It's curly now.

A	drop	B	draw
C	dress	D	drive

2 Let me _____ your attention to this bar chart.

A	loyal	B	political
C	visual	D	official

3 Whatever happens, we will be _____ to the king!

A	careless	B	charming
C	childproof	D	cross

4 He is so _____ that everybody likes him.

A	last	B	learn
C	leave	D	lose

5 If I'm out when you call, just _____ a message.

A	apprentice	B	appointment
C	application	D	appearance

6 Her dog had the _____ of a wolf.

1

New words ▶ p. 7

We like him – he's strange but _____.	Wir mögen ihn – er ist seltsam, aber **liebenswert**
The ice is too _____ to walk on.	Das Eis ist zu **dünn**, um darauf zu laufen.
Put on a _____ pullover – it's really cold!	Zieh einen **dicken** Pullover an – es ist sehr kalt!
She smiled _____ a friendly _____.	Sie lächelte auf eine freundliche **Art** und **Weise**.
Did you hear the new _____ of *West Street*?	Hast du die neue **Folge** von *West Street* gehört?
'Nice dress!' is a simple _____.	„Schönes Kleid!" ist ein einfacher **Anmachspruch**.
I fancy him – how can I _____ him ____ ?	Ich steh auf ihn – wie kann ich ihn **anquatschen**?

2 Crossword

Trage die Übersetzungen der deutschen Wörter ins Rätsel ein.

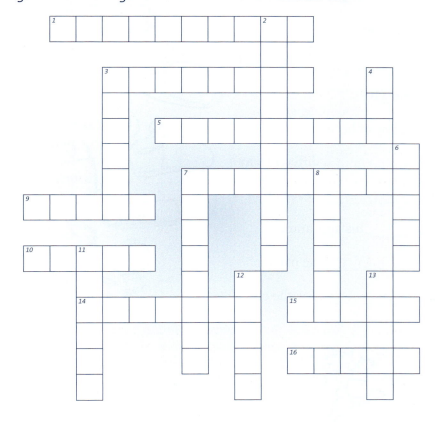

Across
- (1) Aussehen, Erscheinung
- (3) charmant
- (5) Schlafsaal
- (7) anstrengend, stressig
- (9) (ein) Drittel
- (10) verursachen
- (14) liebenswert
- (15) lagern
- (16) herrisch

Down
- (2) Selbstvertrauen/ Zuversicht
- (3) Krebs
- (4) versuchen
- (6) Dia/Folie
- (7) geeignet, passend
- (8) geheim
- (11) anders als
- (12) reagieren
- (13) sich kleiden

3 Odd word out

Ein Wort passt nicht. Finde und unterstreiche es.

1 talk – chat – speak – draw

2 thin – large – huge – big

3 curly – social – straight – blond

4 baggy – tight – torn – loyal

5 peanut – apple – banana – orange

6 fancy – hate – like – love

7 lovable – arrogant – charming – nice

8 (to) book – reception – checkpoint – check in

New words ▶ p. 8

Can a cat _____ with a dog?	Kann sich eine Katze mit einem Hund **anfreunden**?
I have no ideas. You _____ something!	Ich habe keine Ideen. **Schlag** du mal was **vor**!
They won't let you play? That's _____ !	Sie lassen dich nicht mitspielen? Das ist **gemein**!
I found myself in a difficult _____ .	Ich befand mich in einer schwierigen **Lage**.
We'll go by bike _____ taking the car.	Wir fahren mit dem Fahrrad **statt** mit dem Auto.
I don't like rice. I'll have pasta _____ .	Reis mag ich nicht. Ich nehme **stattdessen** Nudeln.

4 Lost words

Ergänze die Sätze mit der jeweils korrekten Präposition. Bei einem der Sätze bleibt die Lücke leer.

1 We made friends _____ lots of great people.
2 This year we're going to Portugal instead _____ Spain.
3 She's so funny – I like her sense _____ humour!
4 Can you lend _____ me £10?
5 He's quite tall _____ a boy of his age.
6 Can you perhaps explain it _____ a different way?
7 Good friends are usually loyal _____ each other.
8 He should care more _____ his appearance.
9 Oh, I didn't notice you were _____ the party.
10 A motorway connects the airport _____ the city.

about, at, with, to, in, for, of, of, to

5 What are the words?

Wie übersetzt man die fettgedruckten Wörter ins Deutsche?

1 We were **on the way** to London.

2 They served us in **a friendly way**.

3 I think we're going **the wrong way**.

4 There's a mistake **in line** two of the article.

5 I can't think of a good **chat-up line**.

6 Which **underground line** goes to the airport?

New words ▶ p. 9

Why did she _____ with her boyfriend?	Warum hat sie **sich** von ihrem Freund **getrennt**?
It didn't work out – I _____ things _____ !	Es hat nicht geklappt – ich habe **alles vermasselt**!
Please tell me _____ you can come or not.	Bitte sag mir, **ob** du kommen kannst oder nicht.
I hate it when you _____ with other boys!	Ich hasse es, wenn du mit anderen Jungen **flirtest**!
So you love her – _____ her about it?	Du liebst sie also – **warum sagst** du es ihr **nicht**?
I was happy when I passed the _____ .	Ich war froh, als ich die **Prüfung** bestanden hatte.
Sorry, could you _____ that, please?	Verzeihung, könnten Sie das bitte **wiederholen**?

6 Two-part verbs

Vervollständige die Sätze mit einem passenden Wort von den USB-Sticks.

1 I feel bad – I think I always mess things _____ .
2 Come _____ ! It's time to go now.
3 She broke _____ with Dan last week.
4 He got _____ the bus and ran away.
5 Now she's going _____ with Jo.
6 She chatted him _____ at a disco.
7 Then he asked her _____ for a pizza.
8 I put _____ my glasses to read the menu.
9 At the weekend I hang _____ with my friends.
10 Why don't you turn _____ the TV if you aren't watching it?

7 Making new words

Bilde aus den Buchstaben des Wortes so viele neue Wörter wie möglich. Wenn du zehn Wörter findest: nicht schlecht. 15 Wörter: sehr gut. 20 oder mehr Wörter: absolute Spitze!

act, ice,

attractive

New words ▶ pp. 10–11

He burnt his _____ when he was eating pizza.	Er hat sich beim Pizzaessen die **Zunge** verbrannt.
I _____ that you all have mobile phones.	Ich **nehme an**, dass ihr alle Handys habt.
She should work harder – she's too _____ .	Sie sollte härter arbeiten – sie ist zu **faul**.
He _____ my name in his book.	Er **erwähnte** meinen Namen in seinem Buch.
The DJ tried to _____ the party _____ .	Der DJ versuchte, die Party **in Gang** zu **halten**.
Sorry, I didn't _____ your name.	Ich habe Ihren Namen leider nicht **verstanden**.
It's the best restaurant _____ here.	Es ist das beste Restaurant hier **in der Gegend**.
My dad _____ me to become a chef.	Mein Vater **ermutigte** mich, Koch zu werden.

8 Verb forms

Ergänze die Tabelle der unregelmäßigen Verben.

1	go	went	gone
2		hit	
3	catch		
4		kept	
5	break		

6			rung
7	leave		
8		sold	
9			stolen
10	fight		

9 Pronunciation

Ordne die Wörter der richtigen Aussprachegruppe zu,
je nachdem, wie der unterstrichene Vokal ausgesprochen wird.

æ	**ɑː**	**eɪ**	**ə**
arrogant (1)	charming		

charming   last   basic   loyal   lazy   perhaps   lovable
around   attractive (1)   racist   catch   ask   nature
arrogant (1)   shame   hand   calm   attractive (2)   arrogant (2)   contrast

New words ▶ p. 12

A candlelight dinner is very _____.	Abendessen bei Kerzenlicht ist sehr **romantisch**.
He seemed OK, but _____ he was ill.	Er wirkte okay, aber **in Wirklichkeit** war er krank.
The story of *Star Trek* is _____ in the future.	Die Handlung von *Star Trek* **spielt** in der Zukunft.
Who _____ the first *Twilight* film?	Wer hat beim ersten *Twilight*-Film **Regie geführt**?
The film *Troy* _____ Brad Pitt as Achilles.	*Troja* hat Brad Pitt als Achilles **in der Hauptrolle**.
He studied _____ and now works in court.	Er studierte **Jura** und arbeitet jetzt beim Gericht.
The immigrant became a victim of _____.	Der Einwanderer wurde ein Opfer von **Rassismus**.
Lord of the Rings is a great _____ film.	*Herr der Ringe* ist ein toller **Fantasy**-Film.
The film is _____ on a true story.	Der Film **basiert** auf einer wahren Geschichte.
She became _____ and had her first child.	Sie wurde **schwanger** und bekam ihr erstes Kind.
He lost _____ of his car on the ice.	Auf dem Eis verlor er die **Kontrolle** über sein Auto.
Pit bulls are dangerous because they _____.	Pitbulls sind gefährlich, weil sie **beißen**.
The film's _____ look so real!	Die **Spezialeffekte** des Films sehen so echt aus!
She began to feel the _____ of the alcohol.	Sie begann die **Wirkung** des Alkohols zu spüren.

10 Word pairs

Welche Wörter passen am besten zusammen?

1) (to) direct
2) (to) dump
3) (to) earn
4) (to) eat
5) (to) last
6) (to) notice
7) (to) return
8) (to) pass
9) (to) study
10) (to) wear

a boyfriend
a film
exams
home
law
a mistake
money
a peanut
a shirt
for weeks

1

New words ▸ p. 13

Nine _____ ten people didn't know the film.	Neun **von** zehn Leuten kannten den Film nicht.
In Christian _____ there is only one God.	In der christlichen **Religion** gibt es nur einen Gott.
Is there _____ life on other planets?	Gibt es **intelligentes** Leben auf anderen Planeten?
I'll do it as soon as possible – just be _____!	Ich mache es so bald wie möglich – sei **geduldig**!
Give her more time – you're too _____.	Gib ihr mehr Zeit – du bist zu **ungeduldig**.

11 Words with different meanings

Finde auf der Liste (Seestern-Magnet) ein passendes Wort zu den beiden Sätzen/Satzteilen auf den Zetteln 1 – 9. Trage es dort ein und unterstreiche die beiden deutschen Entsprechungen.

1)
a) Er schaute sie auf seltsame <u>Art und Weise</u> an.
b) Wir gehen in die falsche <u>Richtung</u>!
__way__

2)
a) Das ist gegen das Gesetz!
b) Nach der Schule will sie Jura studieren.
_____

3)
a) Letzte Woche war ich im Kino.
b) Wie lang hat der Film gedauert?
_____

4)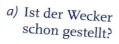
a) Ist der Wecker schon gestellt?
b) Der Film spielt in Australien.
_____

5)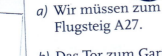
a) Wir müssen zum Flugsteig A27.
b) Das Tor zum Garten ist immer offen.
_____

catch
gate
introduce
kind
last
law
mean
set
__way__

6)
a) Wir möchten ein anderes Thema einführen.
b) Wirst du mich deinen Eltern vorstellen?
_____

7)
a) Was für eine Art von Musik machen sie?
b) Das war wirklich nett von dir!
_____

8)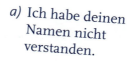
a) Ich habe deinen Namen nicht verstanden.
b) Haben sie den Dieb gefangen?
_____

9)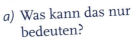
a) Was kann das nur bedeuten?
b) Dein Bruder ist aber gemein!
_____

12 More about ... Great love films

Vervollständige den Text mit den passenden Wörtern aus der Box.

and – at – by – directed – middle – much – on – published – set – still – story – which

The *American Film Institute* (AFI) recently (1) _____ a list of the hundred best love films of all time. The two films (2) _____ the top of the list go back seventy years and more. In first place was *Casablanca* (1942), (3) _____ is set during the Second World War and tells the (4) _____ of Rick Blaine (Humphrey Bogart) and Ilsa Lund (Ingrid Bergman). Rick and Ilsa are lovers. Ilsa believes that her husband has been killed (5) _____ the Nazis, but when she finds out that he is (6) _____ alive, she leaves Rick suddenly without explaining why. Some years later they meet again. They soon discover that they love each other as (7) _____ as ever.

The second film in the AFI list, *Gone with the Wind* (1939), is based (8) _____ a novel by Margaret Mitchell. Starring Clark Gable and Vivien Leigh, it is (9) _____ in the American South in the (10) _____ of the 19th century, at the time of the American Civil War. The film, which was (11) _____ by Victor Fleming, won ten Academy Awards (Oscars) (12) _____ has sold more tickets in the United States than any other film.

13 Word friends

Auf jedem Plakat gibt es vier Wörter/Wortverbindungen, die direkt nach dem Verb auf dem kleinen Zettel folgen können. Unterstreiche sie.

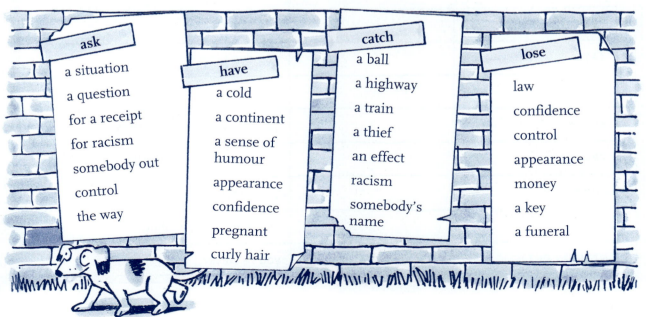

ask: a situation / a question / for a receipt / for racism / somebody out / control / the way

have: a cold / a continent / a sense of humour / appearance / confidence / pregnant / curly hair

catch: a ball / a highway / a train / a thief / an effect / racism / somebody's name

lose: law / confidence / control / appearance / money / a key / a funeral

New words ▸ p. 14

He works as a book _____ for *The Times*.	Er arbeitet als Buch**kritiker** für die *Times*.
Eddie went to the party in his gorilla _____.	Eddie ging in seinem Gorilla**kostüm** zur Party.
He's going to wear a dark _____ to the wedding.	Zur Hochzeit wird er einen dunklen **Anzug** tragen.
He saw the old photos and became _____.	Er sah die alten Bilder und wurde **sentimental**.
The film has won a lot of international _____.	Der Film hat viele internationale **Preise** gewonnen.

14 Opposites

Trage das Gegenteil der fettgedruckten Wörter in die Lücken ein.

1 have **straight** / _____ hair
2 an **intelligent** / a _____ person
3 **fortunately** / _____
4 a **hard-working** / _____ student
5 a **thin** / _____ book
6 a **thin** / _____ cat
7 he's **like** / _____ his brother
8 an **attractive** / _____ girl
9 a **patient** / an _____ child
10 **forget** / _____ someone's birthday

15 Scrambled words: Personality and character

Die Buchstaben auf der linken Seite der Anzeigetafel ergeben Wörter, die die menschliche Persönlichkeit beschreiben. Trage die gefundenen Wörter in die mittlere Spalte der Tafel ein. Die Tipps helfen dir.

			TIP
1	DINK		you're nice
2	ZAYL		you don't like working
3	NAME		you're not nice to others
4	ALLOY		you always support friends
5	TRAGNORA		you think you're fantastic
6	COMATRIN		you show your feelings of love
7	TIPNEAT		you don't mind waiting
8	GIINNLLEETT		you're clever

1

New words ▶ p. 15

The thriller had a _____ ending.	Der Thriller hatte einen **dramatischen** Ausgang.
He lost his _____ on the fastest horse.	Er verlor seine **Wette** auf das schnellste Pferd.
I _____ he can't answer this question!	Ich **wette**, er kann diese Frage nicht beantworten!
We must try to protect our _____.	Wir müssen versuchen, unsere **Umwelt** zu schützen.

16 Word search: Films

Finde 20 Begriffe aus dem Wortfeld „Film" und übersetze sie ins Deutsche. (↓ →)

T	E	R	C	T	O	D	S	O	U	N	D	T	R	A	C	K	A
N	O	S	R	R	S	C	R	E	E	N	E	A	O	M	H	R	A
D	T	S	M	O	V	I	E	S	E	A	F	A	N	T	A	S	Y
H	E	T	C	R	S	N	V	T	A	W	C	A	M	E	R	A	R
S	C	I	C	A	U	E	I	U	M	A	O	I	S	T	A	R	R
C	E	T	S	C	O	M	E	D	Y	R	E	A	R	E	C	T	W
E	P	L	O	T	U	A	W	I	H	D	I	R	E	C	T	O	R
N	H	E	R	O	N	T	E	O	C	O	S	T	U	M	E	S	D
E	A	S	M	R	E	M	E	T	H	R	I	L	L	E	R	Y	A

soundtrack – Filmmusik

17 Words with a similar meaning

Finde Wörter, die das Gleiche bedeuten wie die fettgedruckten Wörter.
Trage sie ein und schreibe die deutsche Übersetzung auf.

1 He's quite **different from** / _unlike_ his brother.   _anders als_

2 Where's the station? – Sorry, I'm not from **this area** / _____ .   _____

3 She should really **break up with** / _____ her boyfriend.   _____

4 Sara is quite beautiful – and **clever** / _____ too.   _____

5 It was very **nice** / _____ of him to drive me home.   _____

6 The Oscar is a famous film **prize** / _____ .   _____

7 I don't know where she is – **maybe** / _____ she's ill.   _____

8 It looks like a boring place, but **in fact** / _____ it's great!   _____

9 We can't say **if** / _____ it is true or not.   _____

10 We have to **get ready** / _____ to go.   _____

18 Definitions

Vervollständige die Definitionen mit Wörtern von dem Laptop-Monitor.
Trage die richtige Lösung von den USB-Sticks in die rechte Spalte ein.

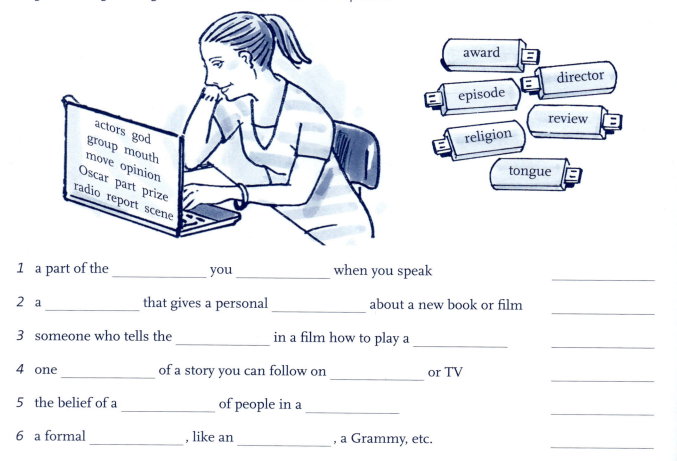

1 a part of the _____ you _____ when you speak   _____

2 a _____ that gives a personal _____ about a new book or film   _____

3 someone who tells the _____ in a film how to play a _____   _____

4 one _____ of a story you can follow on _____ or TV   _____

5 the belief of a _____ of people in a _____   _____

6 a formal _____ , like an _____ , a Grammy, etc.   _____

19 The fourth word

Welches Wort fehlt hier?

1 impressive – impress   attractive – _____

2 Christian – church   Muslim – _____

3 credit card – plastic   coin – _____

4 reliable – character   beautiful – _____

5 speak – tongue   bite – _____

6 house – door   garden – _____

7 politics – political   history – _____

8 fat – thin   thick – _____

20 Word stress

Unterstreiche bei allen Wörtern die Silbe, die betont werden muss.

address	arrogant	attractive	brilliant
repeat	effect	humour	ideal
intelligent	loyal	patient	politics
pregnant	religion	sentimental	situation
technology	unfortunately	unpopular	episode

21 Spot the mistakes

In jedem Satz sind zwei Fehler. Unterstreiche und korrigiere sie.

1 The film starts Johnny Depp as the livable geek.   _____ _____

2 I can't say weather they catched the thief or not.   _____ _____

3 If you eat too many food, you'll become thick.   _____ _____

4 He's very lazey – he just don't like work!   _____ _____

5 The film, which is basing on a real-life story, is setted in Italy.   _____ _____

6 It wont snow, and it won't rain too.   _____ _____

7 We're friends for 12 years now, so I know her quite good.   _____ _____

8 The train is to expensive – I'd recommend the bus instead.   _____ _____

D6 Unit 2

New words ▶ p. 28

Electric _____ make life easier. Elektro**geräte** erleichtern das Leben.

The new games _____ is easier to use. Die neue Spiel**konsole** ist leichter zu bedienen.

Take a _____ and clean your teeth. Nimm eine **Zahnbürste** und putz dir die Zähne.

You can also dry your hair without a _____. Du kannst deine Haare auch ohne **Föhn** trocknen.

It was wet yesterday; today it's _____ again. Gestern war es nass; heute ist es wieder **trocken**.

Dad cut himself with his _____ Papa hat sich mit dem **Rasierer** geschnitten.

You can heat food quickly in a _____. Man kann Essen schnell in der **Mikrowelle** erhitzen.

Please _____ the TV at night. Bitte **zieh** den Fernseh**stecker** nachts **heraus**.

The battery was in the _____ – now it's full. Die Batterie war im **Ladegerät** – jetzt ist sie voll.

Our house is warm – we have central _____. Unser Haus ist warm – wir haben Zentral**heizung**.

I don't like saunas – I can't stand the _____. Saunas mag ich nicht – ich ertrage die **Hitze** nicht.

_____ the oil and then add the onions. **Erhitze** das Öl und füge dann die Zwiebeln hinzu.

1 Scrambled words: Technology

Die Buchstaben auf der linken Seite der Anzeigetafel ergeben Beispiele technischer Geräte. Trage die gefundenen Wörter in die mittlere Spalte der Tafel ein. Die Tipps helfen dir.

	✈		🛬	TIP
1	DAYHIRERR			you dry your hair with it
2	LOSENOC			you play with it
3	INVITESOLE			you watch it
4	WHADERSISH			you use it to clean cups, plates, etc.
5	GRIFED			you keep food cool in it
6	WARMVOICE			you heat food in it

New words ▶ p. 29 (part 1)

We saw human _____ in the snow.	Wir sahen menschliche **Fußabdrücke** im Schnee.
Coal and oil are _____.	Kohle und Öl sind **fossile Brennstoffe**.
Something that burns produces _____.	Etwas das brennt produziert **Kohlendioxid**.
It's an old café with a nice _____.	Es ist ein altes Café mit einer netten **Atmosphäre**.
Tomatoes grow faster in a _____.	Tomaten wachsen schneller im **Gewächshaus**.
CO_2 causes _____.	CO_2 verursacht den **globalen Temperaturanstieg**.
The global _____ is getting warmer.	Das globale **Klima** wird wärmer.

2 Crossword

Trage die Übersetzungen der deutschen Wörter ins Rätsel ein.

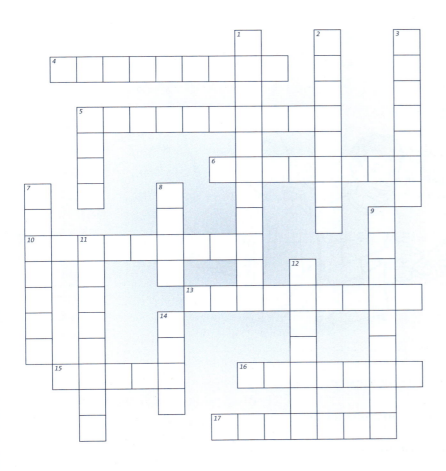

Across
- (4) Fußabdruck
- (5) historisch
- (6) Politik
- (10) Gerät
- (13) Situation
- (15) Ursache
- (16) ob
- (17) stattdessen

Down
- (1) Umwelt
- (2) verseucht, verunreinigt
- (3) annehmen, vermuten
- (5) Hitze
- (7) Heizung
- (8) meinen, sagen wollen
- (9) empfehlen
- (11) schwanger
- (12) geduldig
- (14) Brennstoff

New words ▸ p. 29 (part 2)

He spends a large _____ of money on food.	Er gibt einen großen **Geldbetrag** für Essen aus.
Cars produce a lot of CO$_2$ _____.	Autos verursachen viele CO$_2$-**Emissionen**.
A _____ is a thousand kilograms.	Eine **Tonne** sind tausend Kilogramm.
Most of our body is _____ water.	Der Großteil unseres Körpers **besteht aus** Wasser.
We've missed the sales _____ by 10%.	Wir haben das Verkaufs**ziel** um 10% verfehlt.
We should all _____ our carbon footprint.	Wir sollten alle unsere CO$_2$-Bilanz **verringern**.
Better _____ of the house saves energy.	Bessere **Isolierung** des Hauses spart Energie.

3 Definitions

Vervollständige die Definitionen mit Wörtern aus dem linken Display.
Trage die richtige Lösung aus dem anderen Display in die rechte Spalte ein.

1   the general weather _____ of a specific _____   _____
2   someone who does _____ in a science like _____, etc   _____
3   a _____ that comes out of cars, _____, etc   _____
4   a _____ that helps you with your _____ at home   _____
5   a system for producing hot _____ or air in a _____   _____
6   a house made of _____ where you can grow _____ or vegetables   _____

New words ► p. 30

The wheel was the first great _____.	Das Rad war die erste große **Erfindung**.
A _____ studies the sciences.	Ein **Wissenschaftler** studiert Naturwissenschaften.
The company wants to _____ new products.	Die Firma möchte neue Produkte **entwickeln**.
After school he joined the US _____.	Nach der Schule ging er zur US-**Armee**.
It's great here – I could stay _____!	Es ist toll hier – ich könnte **für immer** bleiben.
I can't _____ the bag – it's too heavy.	Ich kann die Tasche nicht **tragen** – sie ist zu schwer.
Dad went to school in _____.	Papa ging in den **70er-Jahren** zur Schule.
Dad died in 2010. Mum's been alone _____.	Papa starb 2010. **Seitdem** ist Mama allein.
People who eat too much get _____.	Menschen, die zu viel essen, werden **dick**.
A _____ is a thousand million.	Eine **Milliarde** sind tausend Millionen.
We must _____ more jobs for young people.	Wir müssen mehr Jobs für junge Leute **schaffen**.
Do your parents really _____ you to smoke?	**Erlauben** dir deine Eltern wirklich zu rauchen?

4 Spot the mistakes

In jedem Satz sind zwei Fehler. Unterstreiche und korrigiere sie.

1 The earth's atmosphere is made up off different gasses.   _____ _____

2 You need batterys for these games console.   _____ _____

3 Please unplag the TV bevor you go to bed.   _____ _____

4 Better insulation mean you pay less for heatings.   _____ _____

5 My parents are cool, but they don't allow me travelling allone.   _____ _____

6 Carbon emissions is higher today as twenty years ago.   _____ _____

5 Odd word out

Ein Wort passt nicht. Finde und unterstreiche es.

1 tongue – law – ear – nose

2 hairdryer – heat – razor – toothbrush

3 stomach – heart – carbon – throat

4 army – insulation – soldier – war

5 first – second – minute – hour

6 target – power – energy – electricity

7 trash – choice – rubbish – pollution

8 keyboard – mouse – hamster – screen

New words ▸ pp. 31–33

I had to do it – I had no _____.	Ich musste es tun – ich hatte keine **Wahl.**
Wind _____ is a clean source of energy.	**Wind**kraft ist eine saubere Energiequelle.
A _____ creates energy.	Ein **Kraftwerk** erzeugt Energie.
The _____ showed interesting results.	Das **Experiment** zeigte interessante Ergebnisse.
A minute has 60 _____.	Eine Minute hat 60 **Sekunden.**
You look great. – Thanks for the _____!	Du siehst toll aus. – Danke für das **Kompliment.**
_____! You're the winner.	**Herzlichen Glückwunsch!** Du bist den Gewinner.
Use this _____ to plan your holiday.	Verwende diese **App**, um deinen Urlaub zu planen.

6 The best word

Finde das Wort A, B, C oder D, das am besten in die Lücke passt.

A	dark	B	dead
C	dirty	D	dry

1 We had a very _____ summer with almost no rain.

A	attract	B	attack
C	allow	D	advise

2 We want to _____ more tourists to our town.

A	pollute	B	unplug
C	heat	D	reduce

3 We use a coal fire to _____ our living room.

A	apprentice	B	application
C	appliance	D	appearance

4 A washing machine is a useful electric _____.

A	invention	B	invitation
C	insulation	D	introduction

5 Isn't the mobile phone a great _____?

A	emissions	B	conditions
C	situations	D	compliments

6 I don't like camping in these weather _____.

7 Verb forms

Ergänze die Tabelle der unregelmäßigen Verben.

1	fall	fell	fallen	7	fly		
2		bit		8		bet	
3	bring			9			kept
4			read	10		made	
5		chose		11	pay		
6	wear			12			won

New words ▶ p. 34

Can you _____ me _____ this form?	Kannst du dieses Formular **mit mir durchgehen**?
I can't carry the suitcase – it's too _____ .	Ich kann den Koffer nicht tragen – er ist zu **schwer**.
I heat water for my tea in the _____ .	Ich erhitze mein Teewasser im **Wasserkocher**.
Talking about sex was a _____ in her family.	Über Sex zu sprechen war **tabu** in ihrer Familie.
He solved the problems _____ .	Er löste **ein** Problem **nach dem anderen**.
After Grandpa's death, Grandma was _____ alone.	Nach Opas Tod war Oma **ganz** allein.
She looked for the key, but it was _____ .	Sie suchte den Schlüssel, aber er war **weg**.
She _____ not to know her ex-boyfriend.	Sie **tat so**, **als ob** sie ihren Ex-Freund nicht kenne.
He was wearing a long winter _____ .	Er trug einen langen Winter**mantel**.

8 Words with a similar meaning

Finde Wörter, die das Gleiche bedeuten wie die fettgedruckten Wörter.
Trage sie ein und schreibe die deutsche Übersetzung auf.

1 Your room is always **a mess** / *untidy* !   *unordentlich*

2 We don't like this **sort** / _____ of behaviour.   _____

3 Did you ever **find out** / _____ the answer to that question?   _____

4 Is the climate really **getting** / _____ warmer?   _____

5 **Finally** / _____ we were ready to go.   _____

6 Do you need a lot of **equipment** / _____ to go climbing?   _____

7 I like to **ride my bike** / _____ to school.   _____

8 We're lost! We'll have to **ask for directions** / _____ .   _____

9 Opposites

Trage das Gegenteil der fettgedruckten Wörter in die Lücken ein.

1 a **strong** / _____ person

2 a **wet** / _____ afternoon

3 feel the **cold** / _____

4 **popular** / _____ students

5 **receive** / _____ a message

6 study the **causes** / _____

7 **lose contact** / _____ with old friends

8 **healthy** / _____ food

10 Word families

a) Finde die passenden Nomen zu den angegebenen Verben.

1 pollute – _____
2 protest – _____
3 discuss – _____
4 suggest – _____
5 act – _____
6 bet – _____
7 react – _____
8 heat – _____
9 invent – _____
10 cause – _____
11 believe – _____
12 choose – _____

b) Vervollständige die Sätze mit der korrekten Form eines Verbs oder Nomens aus a).

1 The _____ was terrible – almost forty degrees Celsius.

2 The technicians couldn't find the _____ of the problem.

3 Do you know who _____ the helicopter?

4 ManU won – that means I've lost my _____ with Steve!

5 How did he _____ when you told him the bad news?

6 We must stop the _____ of our environment!

11 Lost words

Ergänze die Sätze mit der jeweils korrekten Präposition.
Bei einem der Sätze bleibt die Lücke leer.

1 Jane is _____ the chemist's to get some medicine.

2 Don't forget to unplug _____ the TV.

3 You can only communicate _____ Marc by e-mail.

4 £1,000 is a large amount _____ money.

5 We took the train _____ going by car.

6 He can play nice tunes _____ his keyboard.

7 Dogs are usually very loyal _____ their owners.

8 You can only download the files one _____ one.

9 So tell me more _____ this application.

10 Can you please take me _____ this form?

11 There are seven days _____ a week.

12 China has developed _____ a very strong industrial nation.

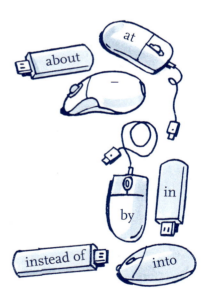
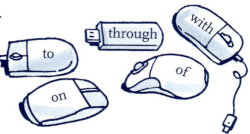

New words ▸ p. 35

Who's _____ for the mistake?	Wer ist für den Fehler **verantwortlich**?
She _____ in tears at the funeral.	Sie **brach** beim Begräbnis in Tränen **zusammen**.
What's the matter? – The light _____ going out.	Was ist los? – Das Licht geht **immer wieder** aus.
Winters in Alaska are _____ cold.	Die Winter in Alaska sind **eiskalt**.
The taxi driver tried to _____ the tourist _____ .	Der Taxifahrer versuchte den Tourist **abzuzocken**.
It's the old story of good against _____ .	Es ist die alte Geschichte von Gut gegen **Böse**.
He has no free time – he works _____ .	Er hat keine Freizeit – er arbeitet **rund um die Uhr**.
A man came to read the gas _____ .	Ein Mann kam, um den Gas**zähler** abzulesen.
Ice will _____ in the sun.	Eis **schmilzt** in der Sonne.
All the lights went off because of a _____ .	Alle Lichter gingen aus wegen eines **Stromausfalls**.
The found fossil _____ of a dinosaur.	Sie fanden fossile **Knochen** eines Dinosauriers.
The dark old castle gives me the _____ .	Das dunkle, alte Schloss ist mir **unheimlich**.

12 Word building

*Verbinde die Wörter 1–10 mit jeweils einem passenden
Wort aus der Mauer. Achte dabei auf die Schreibweise
(getrennt oder zusammen), und trage die deutsche
Übersetzung ein.*

board · conditions · cut · effects · fuel · house · meter · print · storm · wave

1 snow*storm* _____

2 living_____ _____

3 special_____ _____

4 micro_____ _____

5 fossil_____ _____

6 gas_____ _____

7 foot_____ _____

8 green_____ _____

9 power_____ _____

10 key_____ _____

13 The fourth word

Welches Wort fehlt hier?

1 hair – hairdryer hands – _____

2 cold – wet hot – _____

3 time – clock gas – _____

4 bread – food penicillin – _____

5 kilometre – metre tonne – _____

6 toaster – appliances coat – _____

7 hero – good monster – _____

8 art – artist science – _____

New words ▶ pp. 36–37

Even small things can make _____.	Selbst kleine Dinge können etwas **bewirken**.
Temperatures are very _____ in Alaska.	Die Temperaturen sind sehr **niedrig** in Alaska.
_____ energy comes from the sun.	**Solar**energie kommt von der Sonne.
Don't ____ your money ___ something like that!	**Verschwende** dein Geld nicht **für** so etwas
Make an _____ before you write the text.	Mach eine **Gliederung**, bevor du den Text schreibst.
I don't agree with your _____.	Ich stimme nicht mit deinem **Standpunkt** überein.
On the one ____ I'd like to go to the party, but	**Einerseits** möchte ich zur Party gehen, aber
… on the _____, I haven't got enough time.	… **andererseits** habe ich nicht genug Zeit.
Titanic is a good film. _____, it's a bit long.	Der Film *Titanic* ist gut. Er ist **jedoch** etwas lang.

14 Word pairs

Welche Wörter passen zusammen?

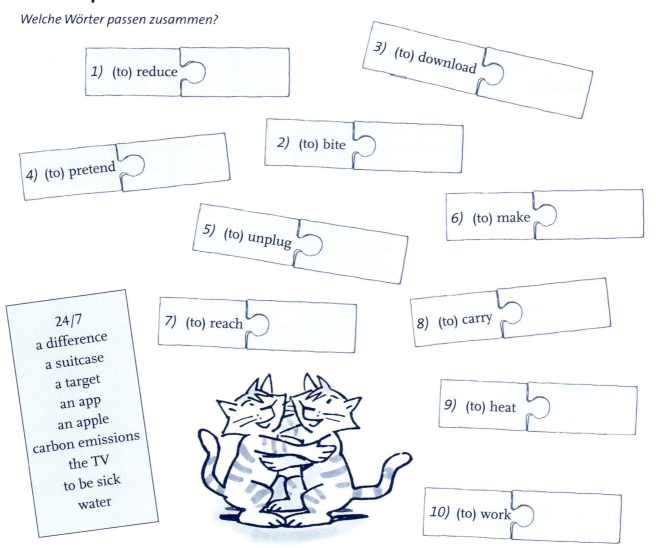

1) (to) reduce
2) (to) bite
3) (to) download
4) (to) pretend
5) (to) unplug
6) (to) make
7) (to) reach
8) (to) carry
9) (to) heat
10) (to) work

24/7
a difference
a suitcase
a target
an app
an apple
carbon emissions
the TV
to be sick
water

15 Words with different meanings

Finde die passende englische Übersetzung zu den unterstrichenen deutschen Wörtern auf den Zetteln 1–9.

1)
a) Sind alle Gäste schon weg?
b) Jetzt sind wir ganz allein.

2)
a) Nicht alle Vampire in dem Film sind böse.
b) Dieser Geruch ist wirklich übel!

3)
a) Die Tasche ist zu schwer für mich.
b) Sie ist eine starke Raucherin.

4)
a) Kennst du diese neue Software-Anwendung?
b) Ich habe meine Bewerbung um die Stelle schon abgeschickt.

5)
a) Gas und Strom werden immer teurer.
b) Bei uns in den USA gibt es billigeres Benzin.

6)
a) Du brauchst nur eine kleine Menge Salz.
b) Ich musste nicht den vollen Betrag zahlen.

7)
a) Warte – es dauert nur eine Sekunde!
b) Das ist jetzt der zweite Versuch.

8)
a) Sie ist gerade nach Hause gegangen.
b) Oh nein – meine Tasche ist weg!

9)
a) Können wir bitte die Rechnung haben?
b) Ich habe noch einen 10-Dollar-Schein.

16 Making new words

Bilde aus den Buchstaben des Wortes so viele neue Wörter wie möglich. Wenn du fünfzehn Wörter findest: nicht schlecht. 25 Wörter: sehr gut. 35 oder mehr Wörter: absolute Spitze!

atmosphere

arm, ear,

17 More about ... Global Warming

Vervollständige den Text mit den passenden Wörtern aus der Box.

carbon – climate – deserts – effects – energy – footprint – fossil – gas –
heating – homes – ice – islands – storms – temperature

The earth's global (1) _____

is rising fast. More and more people on this

planet are using more and more

(2) _____ , which is mostly

produced by burning (3) _____

fuels like oil or (4) _____ . This

sends out a lot of (5) _____

dioxide into the atmosphere and finally leads to (6) _____ change.

But why is global warming so bad? There are many negative (7) _____ . Sea levels are rising

because the earth's (8) _____ is melting. Lots of small (9) _____ , but also low-

lying countries like the Netherlands, are in danger. Most (10) _____ will get bigger because

there will be less rain. In other places there will be more rain and heavier (11) _____ .

Millions of people will lose their (12) _____ , and lots of animals will disappear forever.

Can we stop it? At least we can all try to reduce our carbon (13) _____ . All the modern

technology we use causes CO_2 emissions – so think twice about whether you really need to turn up the

(14) _____ or play video games all day!

18 What are the words?

*Wie übersetzt man die fettgedruckten
Wörter ins Deutsche?*

1 Put on this coat – it will **keep** you warm

2 She **keeps** all her old photos in this box.

3 The printer **keeps** breaking down. We need a new one.

4 It was good to see you again – let's **keep in touch**.

5 I don't need the magazine anymore – you can **keep** it.

19 Two-part verbs

Vervollständige die Sätze mit einem passenden Wort von den USB-Sticks.

1 When does the bus leave? – Wait, I'll look it _____ on the Internet.

2 Bill and Kate have been going _____ for some time now.

3 He feels really bad – he broke _____ with Sue yesterday.

4 Breathe in normally, and then breathe _____ slowly.

5 I can't come to see you – my car has broken _____ .

6 Don't go to that restaurant – they just rip you _____ !

7 Isn't steel made _____ of different metals?

8 She fell _____ on the ice and broke her hand.

9 I think we have to get _____ at the next stop.

10 Global warming will become worse if we cut _____ all the forests.

down

off

out

up

20 Word search: Health and illness

Finde 16 Begriffe aus dem Wortfeld „Gesundheit und Krankheiten". (↓ →)
Übersetze sie ins Deutsche.

H	X	T	B	C	X	H	E	A	D	A	C	H	E
X	O	H	M	H	V	H	B	M	V	M	Q	U	X
O	K	E	H	E	F	E	E	F	N	B	X	G	K
P	A	R	A	M	E	D	I	C	Y	U	E	K	M
E	L	M	D	I	Y	R	B	O	U	L	X	T	B
R	T	O	Y	S	T	U	T	L	V	A	T	C	T
A	G	M	R	T	F	G	N	D	B	N	P	H	D
T	X	E	P	Q	S	Y	T	N	Y	C	J	B	I
I	J	T	O	O	T	H	A	C	H	E	U	W	S
O	M	E	U	U	V	D	J	M	O	G	K	K	E
N	J	R	T	D	E	N	T	I	S	T	U	L	A
D	H	Y	W	O	L	V	U	B	P	K	D	E	S
T	G	G	Y	C	J	M	E	D	I	C	I	N	E
S	L	X	E	T	G	L	V	I	T	J	Q	C	A
M	F	H	Y	O	E	I	J	C	A	N	C	E	R
Q	K	V	I	R	U	S	D	W	L	Y	C	L	K

headache – Kopfschmerzen

_____

_____

_____

_____

_____

_____

_____

_____

_____

_____

_____

_____

_____

_____

_____

D 6 Unit 3

New words ▸ p. 46

Your opinion is important, so have _____ !	Deine Meinung ist wichtig, also **rede mit**!
We should discuss this important _____ .	Wir sollten dieses wichtige **Thema** diskutieren.
Our school has excellent sports _____ .	Unsere Schule hat ausgezeichnete Sport**anlagen**.
Will you be able to _____ at the next election?	Wirst du bei der nächsten Wahl **wählen** können?
_____ ? It's all so boring.	**Wen interessiert das?** Es ist alles so langweilig.

1 Crossword

Trage die Übersetzungen der deutschen Wörter ins Rätsel ein.

Across
- (1) Einrichtungen, Anlagen
- (4) sich verständigen, kommunizieren
- (6) Auswahl
- (10) Armut
- (11) verschwenden
- (12) Ladegerät
- (16) verantwortlich, verantwortungsbewusst
- (18) schwer, heftig
- (19) Gliederung
- (20) eisig, eiskalt

Down
- (2) Herzlichen Glückwunsch
- (3) wählen (zur Wahl gehen)
- (5) Zähler
- (7) jedoch; trotzdem
- (8) Thema, (Streit-)Frage
- (9) reduzieren
- (13) Erfindung
- (14) so tun, als ob
- (15) Ziel, Zielscheibe
- (17) Knochen

New words ▸ p. 47

If there is a problem, _____!	Wenn es ein Problem gibt, **sag deine Meinung**!
Global _____ is growing, especially with China.	Der globale **Handel** wächst, vor allem mit China.
Leave your new mobile _____ for 12 hours.	Lass dein neues Handy 12 Stunden **am Netz**.
It takes an hour to _____ the laptop.	Es dauert eine Stunde, um den Laptop zu **laden**.
Finally her greatest _____ came true.	Schließlich wurde ihr größter **Wunsch** wahr.
_____ is always better than war.	**Frieden** ist immer besser als Krieg.
The local _____ was elected to parliament.	Der Lokal**politiker** wurde ins Parlament gewählt.
She's started a _____ for animal rights.	Sie hat eine **Kampagne** für Tierrechte gestartet.
I went to the _____ to protest.	Ich ging zur **Demonstration**, um zu protestieren.
They started a _____ against the motorway.	Sie starteten eine **Petition** gegen die Autobahn.

2 Lost words

Ergänze die Sätze mit der jeweils korrekten Präposition.
Bei einem der Sätze bleibt die Lücke leer.

1 Too many people in this world live _____ poverty.

2 We shouldn't waste money _____ things we don't need.

3 The air is made up _____ different gases.

4 Shouldn't we all care _____ the environment?

5 They've reduced the price _____ £59 to £39.

6 Our country does a lot of trade _____ the USA.

7 Are you going to sign _____ the petition?

about of on with in from

3 Opposites

Trage das Gegenteil der fettgedruckten
Wörter in die Lücken ein.

1 **agree** / _____ with someone

2 an **evil** / a _____ man

3 have **high** / _____ temperatures

4 a time of **war** / _____

5 I can't sleep in this **cold** / _____

6 a **poor** / _____ country

7 on the **one** / _____ hand

8 a **thick** / _____ soup

4 The best word

Finde das Wort A, B, C oder D, das am besten in die Lücke passt.

A	write	B	skim
C	sign	D	waste

1 You have to _____ the petition at the bottom.

A	appliances	B	issues
C	inventions	D	bones

2 Saving the planet is one of the big _____ today.

A	campaigns	B	fantasies
C	bones	D	facilities

3 There are some good free-time _____ in our town.

A	compared	B	complained
C	melted	D	voted

4 He _____ about the food because it was cold.

A	bossy	B	helpful
C	heavy	D	thoughtful

5 What's wrong with Dan? He looks so _____ .

A	charger	B	channel
C	trade	D	wish

6 I can't find the _____ for my mobile.

A	demonstrations	B	piece
C	peace	D	pence

7 People say it's a question of war or _____ .

A	headline	B	hotline
C	online	D	outline

8 Your essay will be better if you make an _____ first.

5 Word families

a) Finde die passenden Nomen zu den angegebenen Adjektiven.

1 different – _____

2 religious – _____

3 political – _____

4 confident – _____

5 solar – _____

6 poor – _____

7 racist – _____

8 real – _____

9 dramatic – _____

10 attractive – _____

11 strong – _____

12 happy – _____

b) Vervollständige die Sätze mit der korrekten Form eines Adjektivs oder Nomens aus a).

1 There's a danger of getting skin cancer if you spend too long in the _____ !

2 She reads the Bible, goes to church and is very _____ .

3 Does it make a _____ whether I vote or not?

4 Please tell us one of your _____ and one of your weaknesses.

5 Is it better to get an artificial Christmas tree or a _____ one?

New words ▶ p. 48

Can you _____ if you're only sixteen?	Darf man **heiraten**, wenn man erst sechzehn ist.
He left her. Then they _____.	Er verließ sie. Dann **ließen** sie **sich scheiden**.
He smokes a pipe, but not _____.	Er raucht Pfeife, aber keine **Zigaretten**.
It's very _____ that the oil price will go up.	Es ist sehr **wahrscheinlich**, dass der Ölpreis steigt.
At that time of year it's _____ to snow.	Zu der Jahreszeit schneit es **wahrscheinlich**.
I can't _____ this silly idea _____!	Ich kann diese dumme Idee nicht **ernst nehmen**!
The shy star never appears in _____.	Der scheue Star erscheint nie in der **Öffentlichkeit**.
You can borrow it _____ you give it back.	Du kannst es ausleihen, **solange** du es zurückgibst.
What's your _____ on the topic?	Wie ist deine **Ansicht** zum Thema?
We want _____ rights for men and women.	Wir wollen **gleiche** Rechte für Männer und Frauen.
We will have the barbecue – _____ it rains.	Wir machen das Grillfest – **es sei denn**, es regnet.

6 Two-part verbs

Vervollständige die Sätze mit einem passenden Wort von den USB-Sticks.

1 Please turn _____ the stereo, Mike – we have to go now.
2 At the end of your essay, sum _____ the main prints.
3 It was quite warm, so he took _____ his pullover.
4 If you want to change something, you have to speak _____!
5 I never know how to chat someone _____.
6 Who do you normally hang _____ with?

7 Making new words

*Bilde aus den Buchstaben des Wortes so viele neue Wörter wie möglich.
20 Wörter solltest du leicht finden, aber wer findet über 40?*

facilities

act, castle,

New words ▶ p. 49 (part 1)

_____ when you do it – just do it!	**Es spielt keine Rolle**, wann du es tust – nur tue es!
Every night I was bitten by _____.	Jede Nacht wurde ich von **Moskitos** gestochen.
Men _____ 49% of the population.	Männer **machen** 49% der Bevölkerung **aus**.
The sentence doesn't _____ in English.	Der Satz **ergibt** auf Englisch **keinen Sinn**.
The government wants higher _____ on fuel.	Die Regierung will höhere **Steuern** auf Kraftstoff.
He openly _____ the government for the war.	Er **kritisiert** die Regierung offen wegen des Kriegs.
The rule isn't silly – it's very _____.	Die Regel ist nicht dumm – sie ist sehr **vernünftig**.

8 Definitions

Vervollständige die Definitionen mit Wörtern von dem Laptop-Monitor.
Trage die richtige Lösung von den USB-Sticks in die rechte Spalte ein.

1 the _____ laws in a country or _____   _____

2 _____ that you have to pay to the _____   _____

3 a _____ of soldiers who are trained to fight on _____   _____

4 a _____ that shows how much gas or _____ you have used   _____

5 the _____ of buying and selling by people or _____   _____

6 the _____ that you want _____ to happen   _____

7 an important _____ that people argue about in a _____   _____

8 a public meeting or _____ where people _____   _____

New words ▶ pp. 50–51

Let's _____ now and save the planet.	Lasst uns jetzt **handeln** und den Planeten retten!
GPS is a useful _____ for the car.	GPS ist eine nützliche **Vorrichtung** fürs Auto.
These dirty toilets smell _____!	Diese schmutzigen Toiletten riechen **ekelhaft**!
The office was at the end of a long _____.	Das Büro war am Ende eines langen **Gangs**.
He has the role of _____ in the discussion.	Er hat die Rolle des **Moderators** in der Diskussion.

9 Verb forms

Ergänze die Tabelle der unregelmäßigen Verben.

1	make	made	made
2			done
3		got	
4	speak		
5		held	
6		wrote	

7	keep		
8		had	
9			taken
10		gave	
11	break		
12		meant	

10 Word pairs

Welche Wörter passen am besten zusammen?

1) (to) criticize
2) (to) charge
3) (to) deserve
4) (to) vote
5) (to) hold
6) (to) smoke
7) (to) reduce
8) (to) make
9) (to) sign
10) (to) take action

- a break
- a cigarette
- a meeting
- a petition
- bad working conditions
- immediately
- in an election
- pollution
- sense
- your mobile

New words ▸ p. 52

Have you read Brown's latest _____?	Hast du den neuesten **Roman** von Brown gelesen?
The _____ of the novel is a young teenager.	Der **Erzähler** des Romans ist ein junger Teenager.
Say good morning to him. Don't _____ him.	Sag ihm guten Morgen. **Ignoriere** ihn nicht.
It's only 8 pm. He should still _____.	Es ist erst 20 Uhr. Er sollte noch **wach sein**.
Were you able to _____ the answer?	Konntest du die Antwort **herausfinden**?
He's one of the teachers _____ lessons I like.	Er ist einer der Lehrer, **dessen** Unterricht ich mag.
The thief wants to _____ the money in a field.	Der Dieb will das Geld in einem Feld **vergraben**.
Let's _____ them to a game!	Lasst uns sie zu einem Spiel **herausfordern**!

11 Odd word out

Ein Wort passt nicht.
Finde und unterstreiche es.

1 pen – (to) sign – charger – paper
2 disgusting – evil – bad – romantic
3 appliance – campaign – device – machine
4 novel – play – poem – tennis

5 coat – bone – suit – jacket
6 wish – issue – topic – question
7 same – similar – equal – lazy
8 clever – sensible – silly – smart

12 Pronunciation

Ordne die Wörter der richtigen Aussprachegruppe zu, je nachdem, wie der unterstrichene Vokal ausgesprochen wird.

    ɪ   iː

bill

bill, reduce, evil, disgusting, breathe, deserve, heat, device, creeps, meter, pretend, hit, wish, speak, rip off, issue, freezing, complete, equal, peace

New words ▸ pp. 53–55

You look worried. What's _____?	Du siehst besorgt aus. Was **beschäftigt** dich?
I didn't _____ her with her new glasses.	Ich habe sie wegen ihrer neuen Brille nicht **erkannt**.
It's dangerous to _____ directly at the sun.	Es ist gefährlich, die Sonne direkt **anzustarren**.
The war is a _____ between two cultures.	Der Krieg ist ein **Konflikt** zwischen zwei Kulturen.
Is it really OK? – Sure, _____!	Ist das wirklich okay? – Sicher, **kein Problem**!
Can I _____ with you? It's important.	Kann ich mal **kurz** mit dir **reden**? Es ist wichtig.
I'm so sorry – I didn't _____ to hurt you!	Es tut mir so leid – ich **wollte** dir nicht wehtun!
With the new _____, the car will start again.	Mit der neuen **Batterie** springt das Auto wieder an.

13 Words with a similar meaning

Finde Wörter, die das Gleiche bedeuten wie die fettgedruckten Wörter.
Trage sie ein und schreibe die deutsche Übersetzung auf.

1 We can make a difference if we **act** / _take action_ now !   *handeln*

2 Tell me what you think. I'd like to know your **opinion** / _____.   _____

3 We want to take part in the anti-government **march** / _____.   _____

4 This is a useful **machine** / _____ for moving snow.   _____

5 Sue is always friendly **in contrast to** / _____ her sister.   _____

6 Sometimes men and women don't get **the same** / _____ pay.   _____

7 I don't know where Tom is – **perhaps** / _____ in the corridor?   _____

8 Were you able to **work out** / _____ the answer to the question?   _____

14 Spot the mistakes

In jedem Satz sind zwei Fehler. Unterstreiche und korrigiere sie.

1 Please sing the petition and join our campagne.   _____ _____

2 Some politikers don't take young people serious.   _____ _____

3 He's a popular TV moderator, but he gives me the crepes.   _____ _____

4 Jane always crys so much – I think she's just too sensible.   _____ _____

5 It don't matter if he laughs at you – just ignorr him.   _____ _____

6 Be carefull about what you say in the public.   _____ _____

15 Scrambled words: Politics

Die Buchstaben auf der linken Seite der Anzeigetafel ergeben Wörter aus dem Wortfeld „Politik".
Trage die gefundenen Wörter in die mittlere Spalte der Tafel ein. Die Tipps helfen dir

			TIP
1	TONITONICUTS		basic law
2	MIPER TERMINIS		the top man in the government
3	WONT LAHL		the mayor works here
4	NOWT LOCICUN		a kind of parliament for a city
5	NOLICETE		when you choose your MP
6	TYPAR		a political organization

16 The fourth word

Welches Wort fehlt hier?

1 bottle – fill   battery – _____   6 players – team   soldiers – _____

2 start – get married   finish – _____   7 explain – explanation apologize – _____

3 noisy – quiet   war – _____   8 wine – drink   cigarette – _____

4 small – big   low – _____   9 down – up   asleep – _____

5 closed – private   open – _____   10 science – scientist   politics – _____

17 Word friends

Auf jedem Plakat gibt es drei Wörter/Wortverbindungen, die direkt nach
dem Verb auf dem kleinen Zettel folgen können. Unterstreiche sie.

feel: sick, a target, great, comfortable, a petition

make: sense, a photo, a difference, a mistake, an experience

have: pregnant, your say, a discovery, a word with sb., a cold

take: action, speech, sb. equal, sb. seriously, sb. through sth.

18 Word search: Science and technology

Finde 18 Begriffe aus dem Wortfeld „Wissenschaft und Technologie".
Übersetze sie ins Deutsche. (↓ →)

I	E	M	I	S	S	I	O	N	S	P	F	I	P	L	I	B	H
A	P	P	L	I	C	A	T	I	O	N	U	N	N	T	O	A	A
A	A	P	P	L	I	A	N	C	E	D	E	V	I	C	E	T	I
T	I	M	I	L	E	S	T	O	N	E	L	E	C	A	S	T	R
H	E	A	T	I	N	G	G	T	I	C	O	N	S	O	L	E	D
C	O	M	P	U	T	E	R	A	C	O	C	T	D	A	P	R	R
S	O	L	A	R	I	E	L	E	C	T	R	I	C	I	T	Y	Y
P	O	W	E	R	S	R	M	M	I	C	R	O	W	A	V	E	E
G	A	W	G	E	T	F	R	I	D	G	E	N	L	N	I	E	R

device – Vorrichtung

19 Word stress

Unterstreiche bei allen Wörtern die Silbe, die betont werden muss.

accept	action	apology	army
cigarette	comfortable	company	complain
conflict	criticize	emission	experiment
facilities	issue	medicine	moderator
politician	poverty	public	solar

20 Revision: Word groups

*Ordne den vier Oberbegriffen auf den Laptops jeweils sechs passende Wörter zu.
Weitere sechs Wörter aus der Box passen zu keinem der Oberbegriffe.*

advert – ambulance – ancestor – angel – application – audience – brainstorm –
cancer – candidate – certificate – chemist – colony – disease – interview – museums –
outline – paramedic – purse – pie chart – reference – screen – sensible – skyscraper –
station – summary – theatre – tonne – toothache – traffic jam – underground

Lösungen

D 5 – Erweiterte Ausgabe

Unit 1

1 Scrambled words: Australia
1 kangaroo, *2* the bush, *3* snake,
4 the outback, *5* surfing, *6* barbecue,
7 Victoria, *8* skyscraper, *9* Melbourne

2 Definitions
1 area – government: colony
2 crime – jail: prisoner
3 part – essay: conclusion
4 land – rain: desert
5 stamps – place: collection

3 More about … Australia
1 area, *2* population, *3* independent,
4 desert, *5* Aboriginal, *6* beaches,
7 koala, *8* snakes, *9* sunscreen, *10* cancer

4 Odd word out
1 dolphin, *2* recently, *3* avoid, *4* prison,
5 cross, *6* leaf, *7* outback, *8* shape

5 Words with different meanings
1 bush – Busch (wildes Land) / Strauch
2 area – Fläche / Gegend
3 present – Gegenwart / Geschenk
4 cross – überqueren / Kreuz
5 leaves – Blätter / fährt ab
6 by – um / mit

6 Word pairs
1 wear jeans
2 become independent
3 attach photos
4 join a club
5 put on sunscreen
6 die of cancer
7 give advice
8 make mistakes
9 do business
10 ride a motorbike

7 Word building
1 coral reef – Korallenriff
2 lifeguard – Rettungsschwimmer/in
3 pocket money - Taschengeld
4 pie chart – Tortendiagramm
5 newspaper – Zeitung
6 couch potato – Stubenhocker/in
7 stomach ache – Bauchweh
8 motorbike – Motorrad
9 timetable – Stundenplan
10 sleeping bag – Schlafsack

8 Word friends
do: the homework, a good job, business with sb.
wear: a cap, make-up, a ring
get: advice, help, cancer
have: a barbecue, a disease, breakfast

9 The best word
1D borrow, *2C* ancestors, *3C* owner,
4D surprising, *5B* nearly, *6A* witness,
7D settled, *8B* seat

10 Opposites
1 lend, *2* outdoors, *3* nowhere,
4 calm, *5* flat, *6* modern,
7 arrival, *8* fast, *9* little,
10 rising, *11* back, *12* poor,
13 less, *14* illegal, *15* disadvantage,
16 pull, *17* wrong, *18* dirty,
19 remember, *20* weak

11 Spot the mistakes
1 <u>It gives</u>: There are, <u>much</u>: many
2 <u>at</u>: by, <u>percentage</u>: per cent
3 <u>me</u>: myself, <u>too</u>: either
4 <u>borrow</u>: lend, <u>an other</u>: another
5 <u>you</u>: your, <u>spent</u>: spend

12 Making new words
einige mögliche Wörter:
a, act, active, actor, air, an, anti, are, art,
as, at, ate, can, canoe, car, care, case, cat,
cave, cent, coast, coin, contain, cost, cover,
ear, earn, east, eat, ice, in, into, is, it, its,
nation, native, near, neat, nice, no, noise,
nose, not, note, notice, ocean, on, once,
one, onion, onto, or, over, race, racist, rain,
raise, ran, reason, rent, rest, rice, rise,
risen, rose, sat, save, scan, score, sea, seat,
section, sent, set, since, sir, sit, so, son,
soon, sore, sort, star, stone, tea, tear, to,
toe, too, tore, torn, train, version,
voice, vote

13 The fourth word

1 unkind, 2 belief, 3 unconscious,
4 cattle, 5 breathe, 6 poisonous,
7 back, 8 whale, 9 nowhere,
10 bleed

14 Pronunciation

ə Aborigine, ancestor, apologize (2),
because of, colony (2), introduce,
poison, prison

ɒ apologize (1), borrow, colony (1), conscious,
cross, dolphin, historical, honest

Unit 2

1 The best word

1 D information, 2 C make,
3 C training, 4 A needn't,
5 B began, 6 C after, 7 A skills

2 The fourth word

1 letter, 2 sporty, 3 calm,
4 organized, 5 artistic,
6 decision, 7 serve, 8 adviser

3 Lost words

1 to, 2 about, 3 –, 4 of,
5 into, 6 for, 7 –, 8 on

4 Spot the mistakes

1 to work: working, times: hours
2 advices: advice, repare: repair
3 make-up artist: a make-up artist, good: well
4 spended: spent, for: on
5 make: do, 'm serving: serve

5 Word pairs

1 advise customers
2 earn money
3 organized crime
4 plant a tree
5 a poisonous snake
6 print an article
7 a reliable car
8 respect an opinion
9 solve a problem
10 work long hours

6 Scrambled words: Describing people

1 confident, 2 energetic, 3 calm,
4 sporty, 5 punctual, 6 artistic,
7 reliable, 8 logical

7 Word search: Jobs

S	X	A	F	A	R	M	E	R	H	J	D	E	N	T	I	S	T	Q	H
M	B	D	E	T	J	N	U	R	S	E	Z	P	P	A	I	N	T	E	R
E	B	O	B	U	I	L	D	E	R	Z	L	K	Z	L	P	D	C	E	T
C	J	C	A	P	H	K	L	N	C	H	E	F	M	N	C	N	L	L	E
H	M	T	C	A	J	F	Z	G	C	W	V	A	D	V	I	S	E	R	C
A	I	O	U	R	N	A	L	I	S	T	V	E	T	L	W	V	A	T	H
N	K	R	Z	A	G	L	B	N	X	I	Z	P	Y	M	B	B	N	E	N
I	Z	H	Q	M	L	U	B	E	D	I	T	O	R	K	P	I	E	A	I
C	Z	A	S	E	C	A	R	E	T	A	K	E	R	X	I	M	R	C	C
F	Z	C	Q	D	Y	F	I	R	E	M	A	N	R	H	L	B	W	H	I
T	F	K	L	I	C	L	G	Z	P	O	L	I	C	E	M	A	N	E	A
D	T	Q	A	C	T	O	R	Z	Z	K	G	D	X	T	Q	M	C	R	N

actor – Schauspieler/in
adviser – Berater/in
builder – Bauarbeiter/in
caretaker – Hausmeister/in
chef – Koch/Köchin
cleaner – Putzfrau/mann
dentist – Zahnarzt/ärztin
doctor – Arzt/Ärztin
editor – Redakteur/in
engineer – Ingenieur/in
farmer – Landwirt/in
fireman – Feuerwehrmann
journalist – Journalist/in
mechanic – Mechaniker/in
nurse – Krankenpfleger/in
painter – Maler/in
paramedic – Sanitäter/in
policeman – Polizist
teacher – Lehrer/in
technician – Techniker/in
vet – Tierarzt/ärztin

8 Word families

a) 1 breathe, 2 respect, 3 believe,
4 advise, 5 apply, 6 train,
7 decide, 8 introduce, 9 plant,
10 bleed, 11 rent, 12 apologize

b) 1 apologize, 2 introduce, 3 plant,
4 rent, 5 apply, 6 breathe,
7 respect, 8 train

9 Odd word out

1 nature, 2 cattle, 3 postcode,
4 chef, 5 level, 6 ink,
7 garage, 8 similar

10 Word stress

address – advertise – advertisement – application –
certificate – confident – decision – enclose –
garage – indoors – nationality – nature –
normal – organized – qualification – reference –
reliable – similar – technical – technology

11 More about ... Networks on the Internet
1 join, 2 profiles, 3 opinions,
4 suitable, 5 dangerous, 6 application,
7 interview, 8 candidates, 9 impress,
10 cheeky, 11 look, 12 reliable

12 Opposites
1 indoors, 2 confident, 3 out, 4 late,
5 right, 6 borrow, 7 birth, 8 weakness,
9 unfair, 10 complicated

13 Word building
1 racing car – Rennwagen
2 primary school – Grundschule
3 work experience – Praktikum
4 postcode – Postleitzahl
5 first name – Vorname
6 office worker – Büroangestellte(r)
7 waterproof – wasserfest
8 sweetheart – Liebling
9 childcare – Kinderbetreuung
10 driving licence – Führerschein

14 Two-part verbs
1 up, 2 off, 3 up, 4 off, 5 out, 6 off,
7 on, 8 out, 9 up, 10 on, 11 out, 12 on

15 Words with different meanings
1 back – Rücken / zurück
2 happy – gern bereit / glücklich
3 run – leiten / laufen
4 carefully – aufmerksam / sorgfältig
5 definite – fest / endgültig
6 tie – binden / Krawatte

16 Crossword

17 Word groups
jobs
chef, customer adviser, mechanic,
nurse, travel agent, vet
character
ambitious, cheeky, greedy,
helpful, punctual, reliable
a job application
advert, certificate, CV, enclose,
form, reference
a job interview
assess, candidate, impress,
prepare, questions, tie

Unit 3

1 Word friends
do: well, a project, a certificate
go: well, with sth., out with sb.
make: a mess, a deal, problems
take: place, a break, a breath

2 Crossword

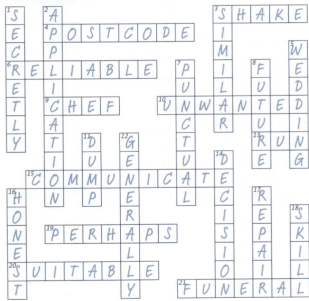

3 The best word
1 A by, 2 C impressed, 3 C only,
4 D ban, 5 A ridiculous, 6 B dumped

4 Odd word out
1 busy, 2 public, 3 go by,
4 greedy, 5 sheet, 6 communication,
7 unwanted, 8 dump, 9 secretly,
10 college

5 Words with different meanings
1 save – abspeichern / retten
2 court – (Tennis)platz / Gericht
3 enter – betreten / eingeben
4 note – (Geld)schein / Notiz
5 miss – vermissen / verpassen
6 mean – bedeuten / meinen

6 Making new words
einige mögliche Wörter:
a, ad, an, and, at, ate, aunt, date,
eat, eaten, end, neat, new, nun, nut,
tea, ten, tune, want, we, went, wet

7 Word families
a) 1 assessment, 2 behaviour, 3 punishment,
4 revision, 5 vandalism, 6 success,
7 advice/adviser, 8 safety, 9 imagination
b) 1 imagination, 2 success, 3 save,
4 succeed, 5 behave

8 Word search: Teens in trouble

Z	P	U	N	I	S	H	H	D	Y	L	S
T	R	O	U	B	L	E	W	D	Q	R	B
X	V	R	B	A	N	T	Q	V	Q	U	E
D	T	T	H	R	E	A	T	E	N	L	H
V	A	N	D	A	L	I	S	M	M	E	A
P	P	G	I	X	C	R	I	M	E	S	V
A	R	D	S	G	R	A	F	F	I	T	I
J	I	R	C	F	L	E	R	D	P	A	O
E	S	U	I	B	S	B	J	Z	I	N	U
E	O	G	P	C	L	G	V	K	S	A	R
U	N	S	L	S	H	O	P	L	I	F	T
F	P	V	I	O	L	E	N	C	E	Y	F
Z	M	S	N	U	W	F	I	G	H	T	B
N	J	A	E	B	U	L	L	Y	I	N	G

ban – sperren, verbieten
behaviour – Verhalten
bullying – Tyrannisieren
crime – Verbrechen
discipline – Disziplin
drugs – Drogen
fight – Schlägerei
graffiti – Graffiti
prison – Gefängnis
punish – bestrafen
rules – Regeln
shoplift – Ladendiebstahl begehen
threaten – bedrohen
trouble – Ärger
vandalism – Vandalismus
violence – Gewalt

9 Pronunciation
əʊ enclose, hold, mostly, note,
overnight, postcode
ɒ alcohol, block, college, contact,
shoplift, solve
ɔː form, more, normal, order,
organized, store
ə community, complete, continue,
customer, instructor, police

10 Words with a similar meaning
1 supporter / fan – Anhänger/in
2 Wait a minute. / Hang on. – Einen Augenblick.
3 mostly / mainly – hauptsächlich
4 fully / completely – völlig
5 maybe / perhaps – vielleicht
6 silly / ridiculous – lächerlich, albern
7 didn't get / missed – verpassen
8 glue / stick – (auf)kleben

11 Lost words
1 at, 2 by, 3 –, 4 in,
5 with, 6 to, 7 for, 8 On

12 Definitions
1 door – hand: knock
2 place – water: spring
3 earth – shoes: mud
4 paper – things: receipt
5 crime – shop: shoplifting

13 Verb forms
1 get – got – got
2 shake – shook – shaken
3 speak – spoke – spoken
4 go – went – gone
5 bleed – bled – bled
6 set – set – set
7 run – ran – run
8 leave – left – left
9 give – gave – given
10 hang – hung – hung
11 hold – held – held
12 make – made – made
13 stick – stuck – stuck
14 lend – lent – lent

14 Word building
1 phone box – Telefonzelle
2 footstep – Schritt
3 alarm clock – Wecker
4 only child – Einzelkind
5 rainforest – Regenwald
6 troublemaker – Unruhestifter/in
7 overnight – über Nacht
8 driving instructor – Fahrlehrer/in

15 Spot the mistakes
1 <u>used</u>: use, <u>of</u>: off
2 <u>such</u>: so, <u>peoples</u>: people's
3 <u>dialed</u>: dialled, <u>on</u>: up
4 <u>shocking</u>: shocked, <u>lieing</u>: lying
5 <u>'m not wanting</u>: don't want, <u>by</u>: –

Unit 4

1 Words with a similar meaning
1 afraid / scared – sich fürchten
2 almost / nearly – fast, beinahe
3 room / space – Platz
4 come back / return – zurückkehren
5 33.3 per cent / a third – ein Drittel
6 full / crowded – voll
7 go on / continue – weitermachen
8 not long ago / recently – vor kurzem
9 enclose / attach – beifügen
10 bus, tram or tube / public transport – öffentliche Verkehrsmittel
11 dirty / polluted – verunreinigt
12 screen / monitor – Bildschirm

2 Lost words
1 on, 2 with, 3 of, 4 by, 5 at,
6 in, 7 for, 8 to

3 The best word
1 B financial, 2 D helpful, 3 A contrast,
4 C prayers, 5 A lied

4 Word pairs
1 adjust to the dark
2 air pollution
3 become wet
4 canned fruit
5 Christian belief
6 crowded tram
7 door frame
8 polluted river
9 secret lover
10 tight jeans

5 Definitions
1 factory – water: pollution
2 difference – things: contrast
3 area – centre: suburb
4 number – job: unemployment
5 person – train: passenger

6 Odd word out
1 Indian, 2 worrying, 3 official,
4 ink, 5 railway, 6 sick,
7 frame, 8 plant

7 Crossword
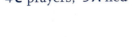

8 Opposites
1 outdoor, 2 tiny/small, 3 disagree,
4 loud/noisy, 5 suburb, 6 inside,
7 unwanted, 8 negative, 9 empty,
10 old-fashioned, 11 ugly, 12 badly,
13 married, 14 disappear, 15 false,
16 sell, 17 weak, 18 worst,
19 unhealthy, 20 polluted/dirty

9 The fourth word

1 turtle, 2 trash, 3 a third,
4 technician, 5 canned, 6 patient,
7 adult, 8 metal

10 Verb forms

1 take – took – taken
2 hurt – hurt – hurt
3 catch – caught – caught
4 hold – held – held
5 build – built – built
6 drink – drank – drunk
7 hang – hung – hung
8 let – let – let
9 stand – stood – stood
10 rise – rose – risen
11 teach – taught – taught
12 shoot – shot – shot

11 Spot the mistakes

1 heros: heroes, peoples: people's
2 've: –, autogram: autograph
3 receipt: prescription, creme: cream
4 colourfull: colourful, impressing: impressive
5 live: lives, runing: running
6 woman: women, interesting: interested

12 Two-part verbs

1 out, 2 on, 3 up, 4 off, 5 on,
6 out, 7 off, 8 out, 9 on, 10 up

13 Making new words

einige mögliche Wörter:
a, air, alone, also, an, anti, are, art,
as, at, ate, ear, earn, east, eat, I, in,
into, is, it, its, lain, lane, last, late,
later, learn, least, let, lie, line, lion,
list, listen, lose, lost, lot, near, neat,
nil, no, noise, nose, not, note, oil,
on, one, or, rain, raise, ran, rate,
real, reason, rent, rest, rise, risen,
role, rose, sailor, sale, salt, sat, sea,
seat, sent, set, silent, sir, sit, so,
son, sore, sort, star, steal, stole,
stolen, stone, store, tea, tie, to,
toe, tore, torn, trail, train

14 Words with different meanings

1 book – reservieren / Buch
2 spring – Frühling / Quelle
3 can – können / Dose
4 lie – liegen / lügen
5 tight – eng / fest
6 order – bestellen / Befehl
7 cream – Salbe / Sahne
8 board – Tafel / Bord
9 bill – Rechnung / (Geld)schein

15 Word families

a) 1 friendly, 2 confident, 3 polluted,
4 strong, 5 political, 6 painful,
7 natural, 8 muddy, 9 racist,
10 artistic, 11 fashionable, 12 weak,
13 free, 14 poor, 15 poisonous
b) 1 poverty, 2 poisonous, 3 confidence,
4 polluted, 5 muddy, 6 nature,
7 free, 8 fashionable

16 Word groups

presentations
audience, chart, (to) present, slide,
talk, visual
at the doctor's
cream, medicine, pain, patient,
pill, prescription
at a hostel
(to) book, breakfast, dormitory,
double room, overnight, reception

17 Word search: Big city life

B	T	M	G	W	T	R	A	F	F	I	C	V	R	Z	V	Z	L	T	Q	Y	N	R	J
P	Q	G	A	H	R	V	O	S	E	T	P	O	L	L	U	T	I	O	N	W	R	T	I
A	I	R	P	O	R	T	V	D	X	K	J	Y	L	O	Y	T	R	U	T	Q	B	L	S
V	V	A	V	T	M	R	T	A	H	T	Y	P	S	K	Y	S	C	R	A	P	E	R	M
E	C	F	T	E	U	A	E	G	S	H	O	P	S	Q	U	T	Z	I	T	S	U	R	H
M	S	F	Q	L	I	M	A	R	K	E	T	F	W	V	Q	A	E	S	L	U	M	J	U
E	K	I	Z	M	D	Y	P	J	I	A	M	C	G	G	Q	T	L	T	W	B	O	D	U
N	S	T	R	E	E	T	T	K	S	T	A	D	I	U	M	I	Y	S	Q	U	A	R	E
T	Z	I	Q	K	E	N	A	I	T	R	Y	S	M	Y	X	O	Y	C	Z	R	E	K	D
N	Q	J	Z	X	Q	O	U	N	D	E	R	G	R	O	U	N	D	B	V	B	U	S	S

airport – Flughafen
bus – Bus
graffiti – Graffiti
hotel – Hotel
market – Markt
pavement – Bürgersteig
pollution – Verschmutzung
shops – Geschäfte
skyscraper – Wolkenkratzer
slum – Elendsviertel
square – Platz
stadium – Stadion
station – Bahnhof
street – Straße

suburb – Vorort
theatre – Theater
tourists – Touristen
traffic – Verkehr
tram – Straßenbahn
underground – U-Bahn

18 Word stress
<u>au</u>tograph – <u>can</u>didate – <u>con</u>trast – <u>cre</u>dit card
<u>dis</u>cipline – double <u>room</u> – <u>fa</u>shionable – fi<u>nan</u>cial
<u>gla</u>morous – ma<u>te</u>rial – <u>me</u>dicine – <u>me</u>tal
<u>Mus</u>lim – o<u>ffi</u>cial – <u>pa</u>ssenger – <u>pa</u>tient
<u>po</u>litics – <u>po</u>pular – <u>se</u>parate – <u>so</u>cial
<u>tou</u>rist – <u>trans</u>port – <u>van</u>dalism – <u>vi</u>sual

D 6

Unit 1

1 The best word
1 B notice, *2 B* draw, *3 A* loyal, *4 B* charming,
5 C leave, *6 D* appearance

2 Crossword
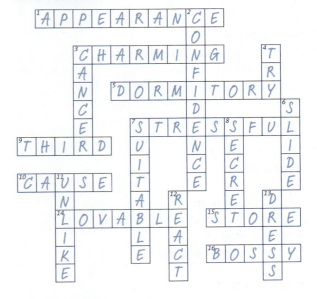

3 Odd word out
1 draw, *2* thin, *3* social, *4* loyal, *5* peanut,
6 hate, *7* arrogant, *8* checkpoint

4 Lost words
1 with, *2* of, *3* of, *4* –, *5* for,
6 in, *7* to, *8* about, *9* at, *10* to

5 What are the words?
1 auf dem Weg, *2* auf eine freundliche
Art und Weise, *3* in die falsche Richtung,
4 in Zeile, *5* Anmachspruch, *6* U-Bahnlinie

6 Two-part verbs
1 up, *2* on, *3* up, *4* off, *5* out,
6 up, *7* out, *8* on, *9* out, *10* off

7 Making new words
einige mögliche Wörter:
a, act, active, air, are, area,
art, at, ate, car, care, cat, cave,
ear, eat, I, ice, it, race,
rate, react, rice, tea,
tear, tie, vet

8 Verb forms
1 go – went – gone
2 hit – hit – hit
3 catch – caught – caught
4 keep – kept – kept
5 break – broke – broken
6 ring – rang – rung
7 leave – left – left
8 sell – sold – sold
9 steal – stole – stolen
10 fight – fought – fought

9 Pronunciation
æ arrogant (1), attractive (2), catch, hand, perhaps
ɑː ask, calm, charming, contrast, last
eɪ basic, lazy, nature, racist, shame
ə around, arrogant (2), attractive (1), lovable, loyal

10 Word pairs
1 (to) direct a film
2 (to) dump a boyfriend
3 (to) earn money
4 (to) eat a peanut
5 (to) last for weeks
6 (to) notice a mistake
7 (to) return home
8 (to) pass exams
9 (to) study law
10 (to) wear a shirt

11 Words with different meanings
1 way – Art und Weise / Richtung
2 law – Gesetz / Jura
3 last – letzte(r, s) / dauern
4 set – stellen / spielen
5 gate – Flugsteig / Tor
6 introduce – einführen / vorstellen
7 kind – Art / nett
8 catch – (akustisch) verstehen / erwischen
9 mean – bedeuten / gemein

12 More about ... Great love films
1 published, 2 at, 3 which, 4 story,
5 by, 6 still, 7 much, 8 on, 9 set,
10 middle, 11 directed, 12 and

13 Word friends
ask: a question, for a receipt, somebody out, the way
have: a cold, a sense of humour, confidence, curly hair
catch: a ball, a train, a thief, somebody's name
lose: confidence, control, money, a key

14 Opposites
1 curly, 2 stupid, 3 unfortunately,
4 lazy, 5 thick, 6 fat, 7 unlike,
8 unattractive, 9 impatient, 10 remember

15 Scrambled words: Personality and character
1 kind, 2 lazy, 3 mean, 4 loyal,
5 arrogant, 6 romantic, 7 patient,
8 intelligent

16 Word search: Films

T	E	R	C	T	O	D	S	O	U	N	D	T	R	A	C	K	A
N	O	S	R	R	S	C	R	E	E	N	E	A	O	M	H	R	A
D	T	S	M	O	V	I	E	S	E	A	F	A	N	T	A	S	Y
H	E	T	C	R	S	N	V	T	A	W	C	A	M	E	R	A	R
S	C	I	C	A	U	E	I	U	M	A	O	I	S	T	A	R	R
C	E	T	S	C	O	M	E	D	Y	R	E	A	R	E	C	T	W
E	P	L	O	T	U	A	W	I	H	D	I	R	E	C	T	O	R
N	H	E	R	O	N	T	E	O	C	O	S	T	U	M	E	S	D
E	A	S	M	R	E	M	E	T	H	R	I	L	L	E	R	Y	A

actor – Schauspieler/in
award – Auszeichnung
camera – Kamera
character – Person, Figur
cinema – Kino
comedy – Komödie
costumes – Kostüme
director – Regisseur/in
fantasy – Fantasy
hero – Held/in
movie – Film
plot – Handlung
review – Kritik, Rezension
scene – Szene
screen – Leinwand
soundtrack – Filmmusik
star – Star / in der Hauptrolle
studio – Studio
thriller – Thriller
title – Titel

17 Words with a similar meaning
1 different from / unlike – anders als
2 (from) this area / around here – aus der Gegend
3 break up with / dump – Schluss machen
4 clever / intelligent – klug
5 nice / kind – freundlich, nett
6 prize / award – Auszeichnung, Preis
7 maybe / perhaps – vielleicht
8 in fact / actually – in Wirklichkeit
9 if / whether – ob
10 get ready / prepare – sich vorbereiten

18 Definitions
1 mouth – move: tongue
2 report – opinion: review
3 actors – scene: director
4 part – radio: episode
5 group – god: religion
6 prize – Oscar: award

19 The fourth word
1 attract, 2 mosque, 3 metal, 4 appearance,
5 teeth, 6 gate, 7 historical, 8 thin

20 Word stress
ad<u>dress</u> – <u>arr</u>ogant – at<u>trac</u>tive – <u>brill</u>iant
re<u>peat</u> – e<u>ffect</u> – <u>hu</u>mour – i<u>deal</u>
in<u>tell</u>igent – <u>loy</u>al – <u>pa</u>tient – <u>pol</u>itics
<u>preg</u>nant – re<u>li</u>gion – sentim<u>en</u>tal – situ<u>a</u>tion
tech<u>no</u>logy – un<u>for</u>tunately – un<u>pop</u>ular – <u>ep</u>isode

21 Spot the mistakes
1 <u>starts</u>: stars, <u>livable</u>: lovable
2 <u>weather</u>: whether, <u>catched</u>: caught
3 <u>many</u>: much, <u>thick</u>: fat
4 <u>lazey</u>: lazy, <u>don't</u>: doesn't
5 <u>basing</u>: based, <u>setted</u>: set
6 <u>wont</u>: won't, <u>too</u>: either
7 <u>'re</u>: 've been, <u>good</u>: well
8 <u>to</u>: too, <u>recommand</u>: recommend

Unit 2

1 Scrambled words: Technology
1 hairdryer, 2 console, 3 television,
4 dishwasher, 5 friage, 6 microwave

2 Crossword

3 Definitions
1 conditions – place: climate
2 research – biology: scientist
3 gas – factories: emission
4 machine – work: appliance
5 water – building: heating
6 glass – fruit: greenhouse

4 Spot the mistakes
1 <u>off</u>: of, <u>gasses</u>: gases
2 <u>batterys</u>: batteries, <u>these</u>: this
3 <u>unplag</u>: unplug, <u>bevor</u>: before
4 <u>mean</u>: means, <u>heatings</u>: heating
5 <u>travelling</u>: to travel, <u>allone</u>: alone
6 <u>is</u>: are, <u>as</u>: than

5 Odd word out
1 law, 2 heat, 3 carbon, 4 insulation,
5 first, 6 target, 7 choice, 8 hamster

6 The best word
1 D dry, 2 A attract, 3 C heat,
4 C appliance, 5 A invention, 6 B conditions

7 Verb forms
1 fall – fell – fallen
2 bite – bit – bitten
3 bring – brought – brought
4 read – read – read
5 choose – chose – chosen
6 wear – wore – worn
7 fly – flew – flown
8 bet – bet – bet
9 keep – kept – kept
10 make – made – made
11 pay – paid – paid
12 win – won – won

8 Words with a similar meaning
1 a mess / untidy – unordentlich
2 sort / kind – Art
3 find out / discover – herausfinden,
4 getting / becoming – werden
5 Finally / At last – Endlich
6 equipment / gear – Ausrüstung
7 ride my bike / cycle – Rad fahren
8 ask for directions / ask the way –
   nach dem Weg fragen

9 Opposites
1 weak, 2 dry, 3 heat, 4 unpopular,
5 send, 6 results, 7 keep in touch,
8 unhealthy

10 Word families
a) 1 pollution, 2 protest, 3 discussion,
   4 suggestion, 5 action, 6 bet, 7 reaction,
   8 heat/heating, 9 invention, 10 cause,
   11 belief, 12 choice
b) 1 heat, 2 cause, 3 invented,
   4 bet, 5 react, 6 pollution

11 Lost words
1 at, 2 –, 3 with, 4 of, 5 instead of,
6 on, 7 to, 8 by, 9 about, 10 through,
11 in, 12 into

12 Word building
1 snowstorm – Schneesturm
2 living conditions – Lebensbedingungen
3 special effects – Spezialeffekte
4 microwave – Mikrowelle
5 fossil fuel – fossiler Brennstoff
6 gas meter – Gaszähler
7 footprint – Fußabdruck
8 greenhouse – Gewächshaus
9 power cut – Stromausfall
10 keyboard – Tastatur

13 The fourth word
1 towel, 2 dry, 3 meter,
4 antibiotic/medicine, 5 kilogram,
6 clothes, 7 evil, 8 scientist

14 Word pairs
1 (to) reduce – carbon emissions
2 (to) bite – an apple
3 (to) download – an app
4 (to) pretend – to be sick
5 (to) unplug – the TV
6 (to) make – a difference
7 (to) reach – a target
8 (to) carry – a suitcase
9 (to) heat – water
10 (to) work 24/7

15 Words with different meanings
1 all – (alle/ganz)
2 evil – böse/übel
3 heavy – schwer/stark
4 application – Anwendung/Bewerbung
5 gas – Gas/Benzin (AE)
6 amount – Menge/Betrag
7 second – Sekunde/zweite(r, s)
8 gone – gegangen/weg
9 bill – Rechnung/(Geld-)Schein (AE)

16 Making new words
einige mögliche Wörter:
arm, ear, earth, hate, he, hear, heart,
heat, her, here, hero, hot, mate, meat,
meet, more, most, pea, pet, post, same,
seem, shape, share, she, sheep, shop,
short, spot, star, stare, step, stop, store,
storm, team, term, there, toe, top

17 More about ... Global warming
1 temperature, 2 energy, 3 fossil,
4 gas, 5 carbon, 6 climate, 7 effects,
8 ice, 9 islands, 10 deserts, 11 storms,
12 homes, 13 footprint, 14 heating

18 What are the words?
1 halten, 2 bewahrt ... auf, 3 immer wieder,
4 in Kontakt bleiben, 5 behalten

19 Two-part verbs
1 up, 2 out, 3 up, 4 out, 5 down,
6 off, 7 up/out, 8 down, 9 off, 10 down

20 Word search: Health and illness

```
H X T B C X H E A D A C H E
X O H M H V H B M V M Q U X
O K E H E F E E F N B X G K
P A R A M E D I C Y U E K M
E L M D I Y R B O U L X T B
R T O Y S T U T L V A T C T
A G M R T F G N D B N P H D
T X E P Q S Y T N Y C J B I
I J T O O T H A C H E U W S
O M E U U V D J M O G K K E
N J R T D E N T I S T U L A
D H Y W O L V U B P K D E S
T G G Y C J M E D I C I N E
S L X E T G L V I T J Q C A
M F H Y O E I J C A N C E R
Q K V I R U S D W L Y C L K
```

ambulance – Krankenwagen
cancer – Krebs
chemist – Apotheke
cold – Erkältung
dentist – Zahnarzt/ärztin
disease – Krankheit
doctor – Arzt/Ärztin
drug – Medikament
headache – Kopfschmerzen
hospital – Krankenhaus
medicine – Medizin
operation – Operation
paramedic – Sanitäter/in
thermometer – Thermometer
toothache – Zahnschmerzen
virus – Virus

Unit 3

1 Crossword

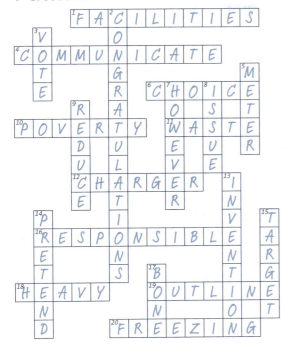

2 Lost words
1 in, 2 on, 3 of, 4 about, 5 from, 6 with, 7 –

3 Opposites
1 disagree, 2 good, 3 low, 4 peace,
5 heat, 6 rich, 7 other, 8 thin

4 The best word
1 C sign, 2 B issues, 3 D facilities,
4 B complained, 5 D thoughtful, 6 A charger
7 C peace, 8 D outline

5 Word families
a) 1 difference, 2 religion, 3 politics/politician,
4 confidence, 5 sun, 6 poverty,
7 racism/racist, 8 reality, 9 drama,
10 attraction, 11 strength, 12 happiness
b) 1 sun, 2 religious, 3 difference,
4 strengths, 5 real

6 Two-part verbs
1 off, 2 up, 3 off, 4 out, 5 up, 6 out

7 Making new words
einige mögliche Wörter:
act, as, at, ate, café, case, castle, cat, east, eat, face, fact, fail, false, fast, fat, felt, file, fist, fit, flat, ice, if, is, it, its, itself, last, late, leaf, least, left, let, lie, life, lift, list, lit, safe, sail, sale, salt, sat, sea, set, sit, steal, tea, tie

8 Definitions
1 basic – organization: constitution
2 money – government: tax
3 group – land: army
4 machine – water: meter
5 activity – countries: trade
6 feeling – something: wish
7 topic – discussion: issue
8 march – protest: demonstration

9 Verb forms
1 make – made – made
2 do – did – done
3 get – got – got
4 speak – spoke – spoken
5 hold – held – held
6 write – wrote – written
7 keep – kept – kept
8 have – had – had
9 take – took – taken
10 give – gave – given
11 break – broke – broken
12 mean – meant – meant

10 Word pairs
1 (to) criticize bad working conditions
2 (to) charge your mobile
3 (to) deserve a break
4 (to) vote in an election
5 (to) hold a meeting
6 (to) smoke a cigarette
7 (to) reduce pollution
8 (to) make sense
9 (to) sign a petition
10 (to) take action immediately

11 Odd word out
1 charger, 2 romantic, 3 campaign,
4 tennis, 5 bone, 6 wish, 7 lazy, 8 silly

12 Pronunciation
1 b<u>i</u>ll, d<u>e</u>serve, d<u>e</u>vice, d<u>i</u>sgusting, h<u>i</u>t, <u>i</u>ssue, pr<u>e</u>tend, r<u>e</u>duce, r<u>i</u>p off, w<u>i</u>sh
2 br<u>ea</u>the, compl<u>e</u>te, cr<u>ee</u>ps, <u>e</u>qual, <u>e</u>vil, fr<u>ee</u>zing, h<u>ea</u>t, p<u>ea</u>ce, m<u>e</u>ter, sp<u>ea</u>k

13 Words with a similar meaning
1 act / take action – handeln
2 opinion / view – Ansicht (Meinung)
3 march / demonstration – Demonstration,
4 machine / device – Machine (Gerät)
5 in contrast to / unlike – anders als
6 the same / equal – gleiche
7 perhaps / maybe – vielleicht
8 work out / figure out – herausfinden

14 Spot the mistakes
1 <u>sing</u>: sign, <u>campagne</u>: campaign
2 <u>politikers</u>: politicians, <u>serious</u>: seriously
3 <u>moderator</u>: presenter, <u>crepes</u>: creeps
4 <u>crys</u>: cries, <u>sensible</u>: sensitive
5 <u>don't</u>: doesn't, <u>ignorr</u>: ignore
6 <u>carefull</u>: careful, in <u>the</u> public: in public

15 Scrambled words: Politics
1 constitution, 2 prime minister,
3 town hall, 4 town council,
5 election, 6 party

16 The fourth word
1 charge, 2 get divorced, 3 peace,
4 high, 5 public, 6 army, 7 apology,
8 smoke, 9 awake, 10 politician

17 Word friends
feel: sick, great, comfortable
make: sense, a difference, a mistake
have: your say, a word with sb., a cold
take: action, sb. seriously, sb. through sth.

18 Word search: Science and technology

```
I E M I S S I O N S P F I P L I B H
A P P L I C A T I O N U N N T O A A
A A P P L I A N C E D E V I C E T I
T I M I L E S T O N E L E C A S T R
H E A T I N G G T T C O N S O L E D
C O M P U T E R A C O C T D A P R R
S O L A R I E L E C T R I C I T Y Y
P O W E R S R M M I C R O W A V E E
G A W G E T F R I D G E N L N I E R
```

appliance – Gerät
application – Anwendung
battery – Batterie
computer – Computer
console – Konsole
device – Vorrichtung
electricity – Elektrizität
emissions – Emissionen
fridge – Kühlschrank
fuel – Brennstoff
hairdryer – Föhn
heating – Heizung
invention – Erfindung
microwave – Mikrowelle
milestone – Meilenstein
power – Energie, Strom
scientist – Wissenschaftler/in
solar – solar

19 Word stress
ac<u>cept</u> – <u>ac</u>tion – a<u>po</u>logy – <u>ar</u>my
ciga<u>rette</u> – <u>com</u>fortable – <u>com</u>pany – com<u>plain</u>
<u>con</u>flict – <u>cri</u>ticize – e<u>mis</u>sion – ex<u>pe</u>riment
fa<u>ci</u>lities – <u>is</u>sue – <u>me</u>dicine – <u>mo</u>derator
poli<u>ti</u>cian – <u>po</u>verty – <u>pub</u>lic – <u>so</u>lar

20 Revision: Word groups
presentations
audience, brainstorm, outline, pie chart,
screen, summary
big city life
museums, skyscraper, station, theatre,
traffic jam, underground
health and illness
ambulance, cancer, chemist, disease,
paramedic, toothache
finding a job
advert, application, candidate, certificate,
interview, reference